BERLIN

BERLIN

Dieter and Anke Adler

CHARTWELL
BOOKS, INC.

CHARTWELL BOOKS, INC.
A Division of
BOOK SALES, INC.
114 Northfield Avenue
Edison, New Jersey 08837

ISBN-13: 978-0-7858-2473-2
ISBN-10: 0-7858-2473-1

© 2008 Compendium Publishing, 43 Frith Street,
Soho, London, W1D 4SA, United Kingdom

Cataloging-in-Publication data is available from the
Library of Congress

Design: Ian Hughes/Compendium Design

Printed and bound in China

PAGE 1: Much of the western side of the Berlin Wall was covered in
graffiti—this surviving section of the wall is typical of the way this
ugly landmark was turned into a means of popular protest by the West
Berliners.

PAGE 2-3: Those who climb the Siegessäule are rewarded with
spectacular views. Here, the greenery of the Tiergarten gives way to the
Regierungsviertel (Government Quarter) and beyond, to Berlin's
northeastern suburbs. *Mike Haworth-Maden*

RIGHT: A pleasure boat packed with sightseers cruises down the River
Spree in the October sunshine. It has already passed the Berliner Dom,
whose copper dome is temporarily without its golden cross. *Clare
Haworth-Maden*

PAGE 6-7: "Trabi Safaris," or sightseeing tours in Trabants, the
notorious automotive symbols of East Germany, on offer on Unter
den Linden, in front of Karl Friedrich Schinkel's Neue Wache (New
Guardhouse). *Clare Haworth-Maden*

Contents

Introduction

Considering that it is now one of the great capital cities of Europe, Berlin didn't get off to a very good start. While the Romans were building fine cities to the west and south that were served with roads, aqueducts and civic centers, Berlin was not even rated as a Germanic hamlet, merely an odd dwelling or two clinging to the swamp-lined banks of the River Spree. By the ninth century, it had evolved into a riverside settlement called "Berolina", which may well have been derived from the Slavic word "burl", meaning swamp. In fact, there were actually two settlements, one on either side of the river—Cölln on the south bank (in the area of today's Museumsinsel) and Berolina or Berlin to the north.

In October 1237, German records first mention Cölln, while Berlin appeared in legal documents seven years later. The local Germanic feudal ruler was the Margrave of Brandenburg, who granted special trading privileges to Berlin in 1251, and to Cölln ten years later. Around the same time, work began on the building of two churches on the Berlin side of the Spree—the Nikolaikirche (Nicholas Church) and the Marienkirche (St. Mary's Church)—both of which still stand today. In 1307, the towns were formally united as a single political and economic entity, although both communities continued to maintain their own administrative identity until the seventeenth century. Apart from the two churches there is little left to remind us of the early medieval city, with the exception of the Nikolaiviertel (Nikolai Quarter) on the eastern bank of the river, surrounding the Nikolaikirche. Although the heart of the medieval city was destroyed in the Second World War, this quarter has been reconstructed to reflect the appearance of old medieval streets.

In 1415, the medieval warlord Frederick Hohenzollern (1371–1440) defeated and killed the existing Margrave, who had led a rebellion against the Holy Roman Emperor. Frederick was duly rewarded with both this feudal title and a new one—the Prince-Elector of Brandenburg. He was the first of the Hohenzollern dynasty to hold the reigns of power in the region—and who would continue to rule Berlin until the end of the First World War. On his death, the title was passed to his son, Frederick II, who established a court in Berlin (the Stadtschloss, on what is now the Museumsinsel). By that stage, the twin town had developed into a settlement of around 6,000 inhabitants.

The Stadtschloss remained a potent symbol of Hohenzollern power, but it also attracted scholars and artists…a succession of Electors attempted to establish Berlin as a center for learning and culture rather than of bare feudal power. The Prince-Elector Joachim I "Nestor" (1484–1535) was a staunch Catholic, but he was unable to prevent the spread of Protestant belief in Brandenburg. On his death, his son Joachim II "Hector" invited Protestant theologians into the city and the city officially adopted Luthernaism in 1555.

Berlin also continued to grow. Joachim II was a prolific builder, although he all but bankrupted his small treasury in the process. As well as redesigning his royal court, he laid out an avenue—the Kurfürstendamm (The Elector's Road) between it and his hunting lodge in the Grunewald (now a western suburb of the city). By the death of Joachim's son John George in 1598, the population of Berlin had grown to 12,000. A visiting abbot said of the Berliners of the time; "the people are good, but rough and unpolished; they prefer feeding themselves to good manners."

To the rest of Germany, Brandenburg was considered "the sandpit of the Holy Roman Empire", a largely insignificant backwater of barren sandy soil, swamps and pine forests. However, this failed to prevent it becoming embroiled in the Thirty Years War (1618–48), a conflict ostensibly fought over religion, but which soon spread into a general war fought to determine the balance of political power within Europe. In the years before the war, the Hohenzollern Electors had done well for themselves, gaining control of the Duchy of Prussia as well as other scattered territories. Unfortunately the Electorate lacked a sizeable army, and found itself at the mercy of its enemies. In 1626, an Imperialist army occupied the city. Pestilence followed, and armies ravaged the city's hinterland. By the time peace was declared in 1648, half of the city's population had died, trade was at a standstill and a third of the city lay in ruins.

However, Brandenburg-Prussia had a new ruler. In 1640, Frederick William "die Großer Kurfürst" (the Great Elector) succeeded his father as Elector of Brandenburg and Duke of Prussia, and he embarked on an ambitious policy of economic regeneration, urban renewal and military expansion. In Berlin, the Elector employed Dutch architects who rebuilt the Stadtschloss and the area around it. In 1647, Frederick ordered the creation of an avenue running westwards towards the hunting park of the Tiergarten. As the street was lined with lime trees it became known as the Lindenallee (Avenue of Lime Trees), which soon became the Unter den Linden.

The Elector's drive to revive the economy led to the abolition of property taxes, which encouraged the

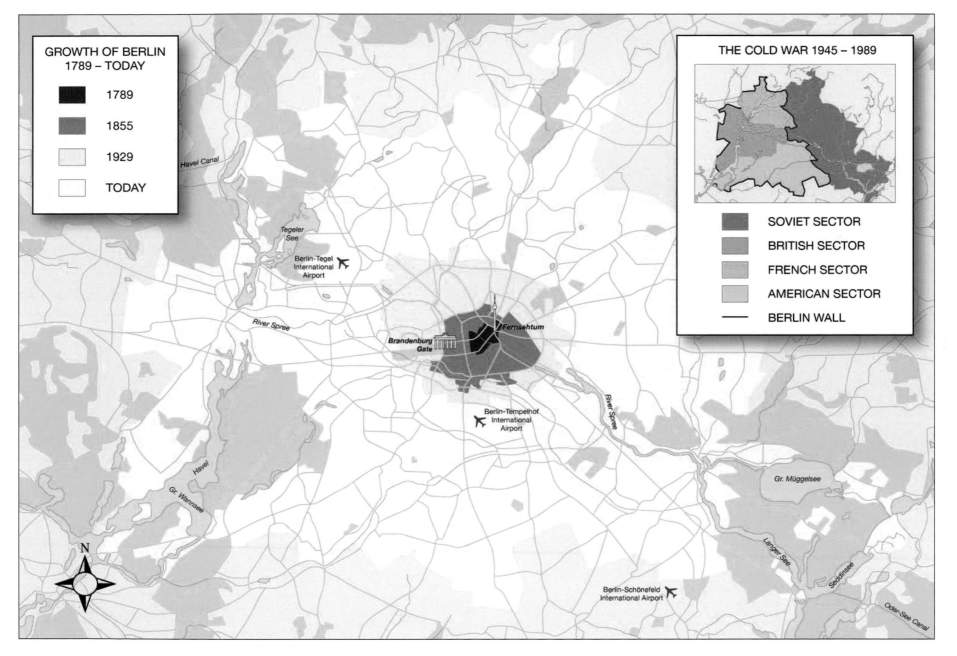

GROWTH OF BERLIN
1789 – TODAY

- 1789
- 1855
- 1929
- TODAY

THE COLD WAR 1945 – 1989

- SOVIET SECTOR
- BRITISH SECTOR
- FRENCH SECTOR
- AMERICAN SECTOR
- —— BERLIN WALL

Havel Canal

Tegeler
See

Berlin-Tegel
International
Airport

River Spree

Brandenburg
Gate

Fernsehtum

Berlin-Tempelhof
International
Airport

River Spree

Havel

Gr. Wannsee

Gr. Müggelsee

Langer See

Seddinsee

Berlin-Schönefeld
International Airport

Oder-See Canal

N

expansion of the city. To cope with the demands of a growing population, he also created the new suburbs of Friedrichswerder to the south, Dorotheenstadt in a bend in the river to the west, and Friedrichstadt to the south-west. To encourage more incomers, Frederick invited skilled Jewish merchants and artisans to settle in Berlin, while his policy of religious tolerance attracted the Huguenots—French Protestant exiles, who soon became an important social group within the city—comprising almost a fifth of the city's population.

By the time Frederick "the Great Elector" died in 1688, Berlin was a bustling city of 20,000 inhabitants, an important mercantile center, and one of the major cities in Northern Europe. His son Frederick III was a superb diplomat and, in 1700, he convinced the Holy Roman Emperor Leopold that Brandenburg-Prussia should be granted the status of a kingdom. Consequently, in January 1701, he became King Frederick I in Prussia, and Berlin became a royal capital. To strengthen his monarchical case, Frederick had continued his father's policy of expanding the city as a political center. In 1695, work began on a new palace to the west of the city—the Schloss Charlottenburg, named after the Elector's wife Sophie Charlotte of Hanover. The architect Johann Nering built a summer palace there, but Charlottenburg was expanded after 1701 to befit Frederick's new status as a European monarch.

In 1696, Frederick founded the Akademie der Künste (Academy of the Arts), followed four years later by the Academy of Sciences. New cathedrals were also built—the Franzosischer Dom (French Cathedral), constructed by the Huguenot community within the city between 1701 and 1705, and the nearby Deutscher Dom (German Cathedral), built in 1705 by Giovanni Simonetti. Both cathedrals were constructed on the Linden-Markt, just to the south of the eastern end of the Unter den Linden. The square was renamed the Gendarmenmarkt in 1773. In 1706, the Zeughaus (Armory) was built a little to the north of the cathedrals,

where the Unter den Linden crossed the River Spree. The building now houses the Deutsches Historisches Museum.

On January 1, 1710, Berlin and Cölln were officially amalgamated, along with the independent suburbs and the united city was officially known as "The Royal Capital of Berlin". By that stage the city had blossomed to a population of 60,000 people. In 1713, King Frederick I was succeeded by his son, Frederick William I (1688–1740), whose sobriquet "the Soldier King" reflects his preference for martial endeavor rather than urban improvement. He had a reputation for being penny-pinching, parochial and boorish, but under his rule the army grew into one of the most formidable military forces in Europe. Berlin was turned into an armed camp, designed to serve the needs of the army rather than the economy. By his death in 1740, upwards of 80,000 soldiers were stationed in or around the city.

The peculiar thing about King Frederick William was that while he built up an impressive army, he rarely allowed them to fight. His son King Frederick II (1712–86) "Friedrich der Grosse" (Frederick the Great) had no such qualms. He succeeded his father (whom he detested) in 1740, and almost immediately embarked on a war with Austria (1740–48) known as the War of the Austrian Succession. The Seven Years War (1756–63) was a far more grueling conflict, but Prussia emerged battered but victorious. Much of this success was due to Frederick the Great's abilities as one of the great captains of history.

While he shared his father's enthusiasm for all things military, he also realised the folly of neglecting the economic and cultural development of Berlin, and the administration of the kingdom. Frederick was regarded as an enlightened monarch and a patron of science and the arts. The Staatsoper (State Opera House) was founded in

RIGHT: Alexanderplatz, or "Alex," as Berliners affectionately call it, has yet to be fully restored to its Weimar-era glory, and is still surrounded by uninspiring, GDR-period apartment blocks. *Clare Haworth-Maden*

1742 as the Royal Court Opera, while nearby the Staatsbibliotek (State Library) helped establish Berlin's credentials as a city of the enlightenment. The architect Von Knobelsdorff also built the Priz Heinrich Palace (now Humbolt University) and a Catholic church—Sankt-Hedwigs-Kathedrale, built in 1747 to serve Berlin's Catholic minority. The Unter den Linden was widened into a broad boulevard, and Frederick hoped to construct a square on its eastern end—the Forum Fredericianium, but it was never completed.

During Frederick's reign, Berlin was a garrison town and, despite the drain on manpower caused by war, remained a center of military production despite a brief occupation by the Austrians in 1757 and the Russians in 1760. Berlin's textile industry was effectively created on the back of the army, while other industries were run by the state itself, a policy which was later expanded to include Berlin's prestigious porcelain industry and leatherworks. By the time Frederick died in 1786, Berlin was a city of 150,000 people, and was widely regarded as one of the premier cities in Europe.

His son King Frederick William II (1744–97) was a conservative rather than an enlightened monarch who, although he continued to oversee the architectural development of the city, cared nothing for its intellectual and cultural status. His greatest architectural legacy is the Brandenburger Tor, designed by Karl Gottfried. It was built in 1787 and was originally called the Friedenstor (Peace Gate). In 1789, the gate was topped by the Quadriga, a statue of Victory riding in her chariot, pulled by a team of four horses.

Despite the conservatism of the King, Berlin remained a center for intellectual thought, and even radical ideas. These radical dreams were shattered in 1806 when Prussia found itself at war with France. In October,

the Emperor Napoleon crushed the Prussian army in the twin battles of Jena and Auerstadt and, on October 27, he entered the city in triumph, his army marching down the Unter den Linden. The royal family fled the city and Napoleon set up a new government, run by prominent citizens. This occupation continued for two years and when the French left they took the Quadriga with them.

In the years which followed, while Napoleon remained the undisputed master of Europe, the Prussian aristocracy did what it could to reform the state. A new city council was elected to govern Berlin and—while the city enjoyed more liberal laws governing commerce, religion and political discourse—the Prussian army returned to its barracks. Restrictions imposed by Frederick William on the city's Jewish population were lifted and, in 1810, the Berlin University was founded by philosopher Wilhelm von Humboldt.

In 1812, Napoleon's Grande Armée was defeated in Russia while the Prussians joined the anti-French coalition the following year. A reinvigorated Prussian army drove the French from Germany in 1813 and, by 1814, Napoleon had been forced to abdicate. A victorious Prussian army entered Berlin and repatriated the Quadriga. Of course, Napoleon escaped the following year and so the Prussians played a major part in bringing about his downfall on the battlefield of Waterloo (1815).

Peace should have brought political dividends for Berlin, but King Frederick William III (1770–1840) ultimately pursued the same conservative line as his father and the state was dominated by repressive laws, secret police and censorship. However, peace did bring some cultural benefits. The architect Schinkel built a series of new civic buildings in central Berlin—the Neue Washe (New Guardhouse) in 1818, now home to an anti-war memorial, and the Altes Museum (Old Museum) in 1840—while the growth of industrialization led to the rapid growth of the city and the establishment of new suburbs to house a growing workforce. By 1820, the city's population had grown to 200,000, but within two

LEFT: The Palast der Republik (Palace of the Republic) in 2007. Thirty-one years after its grand opening, the asbestos-riddled former home of the Volkskammer, the East German parliament, was being demolished. *Clare Haworth-Maden*

decades it would double, to just over 400,000 people.

The impetus for this population boom was the establishment of new industrial workshops and factories. Raw materials from Silesia and Poland were easy to come by, while the growth of the railways meant that goods could be transported easily and cheaply throughout Europe. The premier Berlin industrialist of this period was August Borsig, who in 1837 founded the Borsige-Werke factory that produced locomotives. The suburb he established for his workers—Borsigwalde—still reflects the power of these industrial barons, as does Siemensstadt, a similar suburb built by the electrical industrialist Werner Siemens.

The inevitable result of this rapid expansion and industrial growth was that many Berlin suburbs such as Friedrichshain, which developed into both an area for industry and worker's housing, Wedding to the north and the industrial district of Moabit to the west were all places where living and working conditions were extremely poor. Misery, poverty and disease were commonplace, while the growing class-consciousness of the workforce led to increasing unrest. Political radicalism thrived, both in the coffee shops around the university where Karl Marx was a student during the 1830s and in the cheap bars and tenements of the outskirts. The accession of Frederick William IV in 1840 did little to improve the political climate, and matters reached a head in 1848—"The Year of Revolutions". Demonstrations became increasingly violent and erupted into full-scale revolution in March with barricades being thrown up in the streets. However, by the end of the year, the old order had been restored.

The status quo was maintained until the king's death in 1861, when he was succeeded by his brother King Wilhelm I, who had suppressed the Revolution of 1848. The new king was also a supporter of German

RIGHT: Bombed to bits during the Second World War, the reconstruction of the St. Nicholas Church, the heart of the showcase East German St. Nicholas Quarter, was completed in 1987. *Clare Haworth-Maden*

unification, as was his Prime Minister, Otto von Bismarck. The tool for unification would be the Prussian army which, by the 1860s, was arguably one of the finest fighting forces in Europe. A series of highly successful wars against Denmark (1864), Austria (1866) and France (1870–71) confirmed Prussia's place as the dominant state in Germany, if not in Europe, and in January 1871 the patchwork of small German states were united into a single German state with Wilhelm I at its head, ruling not as Konig (King), but as Kaiser (Emperor). Berlin was now the capital of the German Reich (Empire).

During this period of the Second Reich (the first being reserved for the Holy Roman Empire), Berlin became an even greater industrial and commercial center, and the city enjoyed a boom created by its new status as Imperial capital. The city expanded rapidly, incorporating new suburbs such as Wilmersdorf to the south of Charlottenburg, Kreutzberg immediately south of the center, Prenzlauerberg to the north-east, and Schöneberg south of the Tiergarten. Not all of these new suburbs were slums—some were built under an enlightened new urban plan developed by James Hobrecht in 1862. The Hobrecht Plan for Berlin envisaged the creation of Mietskasernen—well-constructed tenement to house industrial workers, with proper amenities.

This period was known in Berlin as Grunderzeit (The Foundation Years), where pride in the city was marked by vast housing schemes, new civic buildings and in the hectic pace of Berlin nightlife. This was a far cry from the Calvinist values of the eighteenth century, but they reflected Berliners' view of their city as a thriving metropolis. It was during this period that the Berliner Dom (Berlin Cathedral) was built. Later, the Museumsinsel was chosen as the site for a selection of imposing civic museums and art galleries, designed to

LEFT: Alexanderplatz's Berolinahaus was designed by architect Peter Behrens to accommodate stores, offices, and restaurants. Constructed in the early 1930s, it is an example of the Neue Sachlichkeit ("New Objectivity") style. *Clare Haworth-Maden*

rival the other great collections of Europe. The Neues Museum, completed in 1859, was followed by the Nationalgalerie (now the Alte Nationalgalerie) in 1864.

Perhaps the greatest Grunderzeit building in Berlin was the Reichstag, designed by Paul Wallot to symbolize German national identity. Construction began in 1884 and it was completed ten years later. It represented a commitment to democracy and political representation, but election remained the privilege of the wealthy until the collapse of the Second Reich in 1918. In Berlin as in the rest of Germany, the Kaiser still ruled supreme. However, Berliners were allowed the chance to vote in civic elections and, by 1877, the Social Democratic Party (SDP)—founded in 1869—had secured 405 of the popular vote. From that point on Berlin was dubbed "Red Berlin" and seen by conservatives as a dangerous hotbed of radical politics.

However, in August 1914, Germany was plunged into world war, a conflict which was largely the creation of Kaiser Wilhelm II. By then Berlin was a teeming industrial city of four million inhabitants—the military powerhouse of the German war effort. However, the expected military victories failed to materialize, and instead Germany became embroiled in a pointless war that bled her of manpower and money. In Berlin, the effects were felt through food shortages and rationing, while the anti-war movement gained momentum. Troops were used to suppress anti-war strikes in Berlin factories but, by November 1918, it was clear that the army faced defeat on the Western Front, and mutiny spread through the ranks. In Berlin, the Imperial Guards joined the mutineers and, on November 9, the Kaiser abdicated, thereby bringing the war to an end.

His abdication and exile also ushered in the era of the

RIGHT: Julius Raschdorff's formidable-looking, Neo-Baroque Berliner Dom makes the television tower beyond look comparatively toothpicklike. The Protestant cathedral is pictured without its crowning cross, which had been removed for restoration. *Clare Haworth-Maden*

Weimar Republic. Philip Scheidemann of the SDP addressed a crowd in the Konigsplatz (now Platz der Republik), crying; "Long live the German Republic!" Street battles between monarchists, socialists, communists and soldiers continued until martial law was imposed by the SDP, who formed the new Republican government. During the fighting, the communist heroine Rosa Luxemburg was arrested and killed by Freikorps soldiers following the orders of the government—a plaque still marks the spot where her body was thrown into the Landwehr Canal. The German revolution of 1918–19 had been crushed.

The decade which followed was marked by political instability and cultural exuberance. While politicians of various left or center politics argued over Germany's future, and industry was plagued by strikes, Berliners tried to enjoy themselves. It was a city where art and culture flourished and, by 1927, Berlin boasted over 70 nightclubs and cabarets; it had become the center of one of Europe's great film industries, and home to some of the greatest artists and thinkers of the age. Revolutionary ideas in architecture were being developed in the Bauhaus School, and experiments in urban architecture were being attempted in the Berlin suburbs. While artists such as Otto Dix and George Grosz defied the art world, Bertold Brecht's haunting "Dreigroschenoper (Threepenny Opera)" played to packed theaters. Berlin had become the cultural center of Europe, however, there were those who were determined to spoil the party.

In 1923, a former corporal called Adolf Hitler launched an attempted coup in a Munich beer-hall. The founder of the fascist National Socialist Party (NSDAP or "Nazi" Party) was arrested and imprisoned, but the global depression of 1929 led to widespread poverty and

BELOW: Set into the cobbles of Bebelplatz is a plaque reminding passers-by that this was where the Nazi-instigated Bücherverbrennung, or "burning of the books," took place on May 10, 1933. *Clare Haworth-Maden*

bankruptcy with nearly one Berliner in four being destitute. The Nazis offered an alternative to the seemingly pointless arguments of left-wing politics and, in 1932, the NSDAP took 40 percent of the vote, becoming the largest single party in the Reichstag. In Berlin, the Communists became the largest single party, but they were unable to prevent Hitler's election as Reichschancellor. In January 1932, his supporters held a torchlight march through the Brandenberg Gate. Hitler was now in power.

He led a broad coalition of Nazis and German nationalists, and was aided by a refusal of the SPD and the Communists to form an alliance. In February 1933, the Reichstag was destroyed by fire—an act almost certainly conducted by Nazi agents. Hitler used the event to set aside the constitution and called another election. This time, left-wing meetings were banned, newspapers were censored and rival politicians arrested. They still polled less than a third of the vote in Berlin, but in the rest of Germany Hitler won his mandate and, by April, he had assumed dictatorial powers. Berlin was now the capital of a one-party fascist state. By July 1934, Hitler had successfully removed his last remaining political rivals and proclaimed himself Führer (Leader).

A concentration camp was established at Sachsenhausen on the outskirts of Berlin, and political opponents were imprisoned there by the thousand. Next came a clampdown on artistic and cultural expression. Cabarets were closed, "degenerate art" was condemned, and Minister of Propaganda Goebbels organized mass book burnings of "decadent" literature, including the works of Thomas Mann and H.G. Wells. Nazi Party membership became obligatory for all professionals while unemployment was dealt with by means of public works programs and a dramatic expansion of the armed services.

RIGHT: Not much of the Berlin Wall (pictured alongside the Finance Ministry) still stands, for this detested symbol of a divided city and painful past was largely demolished following Germany's reunification. *Clare Haworth-Maden*

Then it was the turn of Berlin's Jewish community. First, Jewish businesses were boycotted and Jews attacked in the streets. Next came the introduction of restrictive laws which banned inter-racial marriages, the holding of public office and the surrender of passports. Businesses were "Aryanised" and, in November 1938, the first Berlin Jews were rounded up and taken to Sachsenhausen. What followed was a systematic destruction of Berlin's once vibrant Jewish community that continued unabated until 1945. In 1926, the Jewish population of Berlin was 160,000. By 1941, approximately 75,000 remained but at the end of the war there were fewer than 5,000 survivors.

The Nazis wanted Berlin to represent the very best of the new "Third Reich", but although grandiose schemes were proposed by Hitler's architect, Albert Speer, little was actually accomplished. In Speer's vision, the city center would be demolished and replaced by a new city hub called "Germania"—an attempt to remove any lingering taint or "Red Berlin". The only aspect of Speer's vision which saw fruition was the construction of a giant Olympiastadion to house the 1936 Olympic Games. It still survives today, although it was extensively refurbished for the 2006 FIFA World Cup. For the most part, the Nazis left Berlin alone, although various civic buildings such as Hitler's Chancellery were built immediately before the outbreak of the Second World War.

The Allies were less kind to Berlin than Albert Speer. The first bombs fell on Berlin in early 1940 but the pounding of the city began in earnest in 1943, when mass evacuations to the countryside were organised. By the end of the year, over 700,000 Berliner women and children had been moved outside the city. This evacuation came just in time as over 10,000 tons of bombs were dropped on the city by the Royal Air Force between November 1943 and February 1944, destroying much of the city center and killing approximately 5,000 people. Over 250,000 homes were destroyed in these raids. Worse was to come—on February 12, 1945 the Allies launched their heaviest bombing raid on the city yet, killing over 25,000 people in a firestorm which ravaged Berlin's industrial suburbs.

Then, in January 1945, a vengeful Soviet army launched its final offensive in Poland and had reached the outskirts of the city two months later. Hitler elected to remain in Berlin and, on his birthday—April 20—the first Soviet shells began to fall on the city. Two days, later the city was encircled and, on April 23, the assault began. Within three days, Soviet troops had pushed their way into the city from the south-west and, on April 30, Soviet troops stormed and captured the Reichstag. The following day Hitler committed suicide. By May 2, it was all over—the Soviets had crushed the last pockets of German resistance. Berlin had fallen, but at a cost. It has been estimated that over 25,000 Soviet troops died during the assault, while German losses were considerably higher.

Berlin was a city in rubble, with no food, no power, and no essentials. It took years to clear the rubble from the streets—Trümmerfrauen (Rubble Women) were a constant sight throughout the city. The Soviets dismantled whatever German industrial facilities survived and shipped them east as reparations while, under the terms of the Yalta agreement, Berlin was divided into sectors, each controlled by a different Allied power. The Soviets controlled the eastern sector, while the Americans, the British and the French divided the rest of Berlin between them.

At first the system worked well but, by 1946, the Soviets and the Western Allies had become less cooperative, particularly after the election of civilian administrators who for the most part were socialists rather than Soviet-backed communists. By the spring of 1948, this lack of cooperation had reached crisis point. In response to an attempt to merge the remaining three zones, the Soviets cut transport links between Berlin and the Western Allied sectors in Germany. As West Berlin was now cut off, the Western Allies instituted an airlift which flew in essential supplies. This "Berlin airlift" saved the city from starvation, but it did little to smooth relations.

In May 1949, the blockade was called off and the Allies linked their sectors into one entity—West Berlin. It became part of the newly formed Federal Republic of Germany, formed from a similar unification of the sectors of Germany controlled by the three Western Allied powers. In October, the German Democratic Republic (GDR) was formed and elected a communist government with its capital in East Berlin. Germany was now divided, and placed at the forefront of a new Cold War. In Berlin, the business of rebuilding the shattered city continued while the two halves of the city continued to develop separately. Essentially much of the old city center was now part of East Berlin, while West Berlin encompassed everything from Reinickendorf in the north through Tiergarten and Kreutzberg to Neuköln in the south. The Western sector also stretched as far east as Spandau and Zehlendorf.

This fragile existence continued until August 1961, when the GDR sealed off the border crossings with barriers and cut the cross-border metro lines. Within 24 hours, West Berlin was completely sealed off from the East. Within days work began on the construction of a wall which would eventually encircle the 160 kilometer (100 mile) perimeter of West Berlin. It divided streets, where one side was now in the East and the other side in the West. The GDR dubbed this an "Anti-Fascist Protection Rampart". To the rest of the world it became known as "The Berlin Wall".

In the years that followed, Berlin remained a city divided; where armed guards and searchlights became the norm, and border crossings were strictly controlled. A tenuous road link was permitted between West Berlin and the rest of West Germany and, when President Kennedy visited the city and made his "Ich bin ein Berliner!" speech in 1963, the West Berliners understood the sentiments he was trying to express. Despite the provocation, West Berlin would remain part of Western Europe.

West Berlin prospered, while in East Berlin the historic heart of the city was replaced with new parks and civic buildings, built in the modern Soviet style. As the old Museumsinsel now lay in the East, architect Hans Scharoun designed a new Kulturforum in the Tiergarten, which included a concert hall—the Philarmonie (1963), and the Neue Nationalgalerie (1968). Both Germanies were turning Berlin into a showcase. What really benefited West Berlin was the influx of aid—Berliners enjoyed special tax concessions and work rates, transport was heavily subsidized, and housing was kept artificially cheap, despite the lack of space within the wall.

During the 1970s and 1980s, the GDR maintained its hard-line stance, particularly with its secret police force, the Stasi, who maintained surveillance files on all suspected of dealings with the West. Then in 1985 came Michael Gorbachev, the new General Secretary of the Soviet Communist Party. He announced that the old ways were no longer working and instituted a policy of perestroika (restructuring). By 1989, it was becoming clear that the GDR would have to reform or face a mass revolt. In October, Erich Honiker was ousted as Chairman of the GDR, and on November 9 his successor Egon Krenz announced the opening of the borders. Thousands flocked through the Berlin Wall checkpoints, marking the end of the division of the city.

Reforms continued apace. As the wall was torn down, democratic elections were held in the East and, in October 1990, German was reunified into a single country. The following year, the decision was made to move the capital of the new German Republic back to Berlin. Unification brought many short-term problems and the economic differences between East and West Berlin were marked, as was the state of the infrastructure. The city authorities now had to bring the whole city up to the same standards, a process which was being repeated throughout Germany at enormous cost to the German

ABOVE: A view from the Siegessäule (Victory Column), looking down the Strasse des 17. Juni toward the Brandenburger Tor. The outlines of Berlin's television tower and cathedral are discernible on the skyline. *Mike Haworth-Maden*

treasury. In West Berlin, the end of the Cold War also meant an end of subsidies and concessions, which led to unemployment and hardship. However, in 1994, the Allied powers officially relinquished control over the city and the German government began its relocation from Bonn to Berlin.

Today, Berlin is a thriving city again where its new-found identity is best symbolized by the construction of a new Reichstag, designed by Sir Norman Foster. Other new landmarks include: the remodeling of the Potsdamer Platz; the historic reconstruction of parts of the old medieval city; the expansion of the Deutsches Historisches Museum through the reunification of its collections; and, above all, the identity provided by the re-establishment of the city as the seat of German government—"the Berlin Republic". The twentieth century was far from kind to Berlin but the signs are that the twenty-first century will see the city develop along new lines, most of which appear to be beneficial to Berlin and its long-suffering people.

LEFT: One of the few surviving stretches of the Berlin Wall stands behind the Finance Ministry, the erstwhile Nazi-era Ministry of Aviation on Wilhelmstrasse and Leipziger Strasse. *Clare Haworth-Maden*

RIGHT: The Sowjetisches Ehrenmal (Monument to Soviet Soldiers) dates from 1945. This memorial to those killed during the Second World War's battle for Berlin incorporates marble from Hitler's Reichskanzlei (Reich Chancellery). *Clare Haworth-Maden*

PAGE 24: The German flag flies in front of the Reichstag's Neo-Renaissance façade. This was completed in 1894, the legend "Dem Deutschen Volke (To the German People)" being added in 1916. *Clare Haworth-Maden*

PAGE 25: The chariot pulled by four horses atop the Brandenburger Tor is known as the Quadriga. The goddess of victory brandishes a staff adorned with the Prussian eagle and Iron Cross. *Clare Haworth-Maden*

LEFT: The Reichstag building, once again the home of the German Bundestag (parliament). British architect Sir Norman Foster's iconic glass dome symbolizes modern, post-reunification Germany and its transparent, democratic government. *Clare Haworth-Maden*

LEFT: The Brandenburger Tor (Brandenburg Gate) has become a symbol of Berlin. This imposing, Neo-Classical edifice was originally erected at the end of Unter den Linden during the late eighteenth century. *Clare Haworth-Maden*

BELOW: The Reichstag's dome is visible from the Memorial to the Murdered Jews of Europe–both modern features of Berlin that evoke its turbulent past. *Clare Haworth-Maden*

LEFT: A Prussian eagle adorns the Weidendammer Brücke, Otto Stahn's 1897 bridge over the River Spree near Bertholt Brecht's GDR-era Berliner Ensemble (formerly the Neues Theater am Schiffbauerdamm). *Clare Haworth-Maden*

RIGHT: Berlin birds take a rest on the massive representation of Neptune that dominates the Neo-Baroque Neptunbrunnen (Neptune Fountain), sculpted by Reinhold Begas, off the Spandauer Strasse in the Mitte district. *Clare Haworth-Maden*

FOLLOWING PAGE: A view of the Reichstag from a vantage point alongside the River Spree. The River Spree, which is around 250 miles (400 kilometers) long, flows through the center of Berlin. *Clare Haworth-Maden*

Hohenzollern Berlin

FRIDERICVS GVILELMVS III STVDIO ANTIQVITATIS OMNIGENAE ET ARTIV

BELOW: The neo-classical Alte Museum (Old Museum) on the Museumsinsel was designed by architect Karl Schinkel and completed in 1830. Until 1845, it was known as the Royal Museum. Today it houses the city's world-class Ägyptisches Museum (Egyptian Museum)

Hohenzollern Berlin

Berlin is a relatively new city in European terms. It may have existed in some form before the Middle Ages, but it never appeared on any map or charter until the fourteenth century. By that stage, other future European capitals such as London, Paris and Rome were already thriving, bustling cities. However, Berlin was the seat of the Hohenzollern family, who acquired the title of the Elector Princes of Brandenburg in the fourteenth century. In so doing, they became feudal landowners whose territories included Berlin and the neighboring settlement of Cölln, located on the opposite banks of the River Spree.

The Hohenzollerns made Berlin their capital, building a feudal fortress—the Stadtschloss on an island in the River Spree between the two settlements. That meant they were well placed to harness the revenue of passing river traffic and protect the twin settlements. The castle was remodeled several times over the centuries which followed, but it remained the principal seat of the Hohezollern dynasty until the closing days of the First World War. In Berlin, the presence of feudal overlords within the walls of the city hindered the development of free commerce, which was considerably less developed during the Renaissance than in other German cities. However, the presence of a vibrant court attracted artisans, builders and artists, eager to benefit from Hohezollern patronage.

The oldest part of the twin settlement was concentrated around the river, and it is here—in the area known as the Nikolaiviertel—where the oldest buildings in the city now stand; the parish churches of the Marienkirche and the Nikolaikirche. Although both the churches and the area have been heavily restored, they still offer some flavour of the medieval and renaissance city. However, a combination of Allied bombs, Soviet artillery and East German urban planning removed almost all original traces of the old city. For the most part, the birth of modern Berlin began in the mid-seventeenth century, when the Elector Princes began laying out new streets and commissioning grand palaces and civic buildings, with the aim of making Berlin a capital to be proud of.

In 1647, the "Great Elector" ordered the building of the tree-lined Unter den Linden, connecting the Stadtschloss to his new palace of Charlottenburg. More projects followed—new districts were added to the city, and magnificent buildings were commissioned. By the mid-eighteenth century, Berlin and Cölln had become a unified and bustling city of 100,000 inhabitants, boasting some of the finest examples of baroque, rococo and neo-classical architecture in Europe. However, the real expansion of the city took place after the end of the Napoleonic Wars in 1815. While the Hohenzollern monarchs encouraged the building of imposing civic buildings and palaces, the growing demands of industry led to the creation of sprawling new suburbs, built to service the needs of Berlin's factories and workshops. By the mid-nineteenth century, Berlin had become one of the most important industrial centers in Europe; a sprawling, teeming metropolis where a prosperous middle class rubbed shoulders with poorly-paid and often disaffected working population. Behind the glittering façade of Imperial Berlin lurked the specters of revolution and extremism.

ABOVE: There is no clear answer as to why the coat of arms of Berlin portrays a rampant bear, but it may well date from the reign of Albrecht "the Bear" (1100–70), the first Margrave of Brandenburg and, therefore, one of the first feudal rulers of Berlin.

RIGHT: The Schloss Charlottenburg (Charlottenburg Palace) was built in honor of Queen Sophie Charlotte during the 1690s, and became the summer home of the Hohenzollerns during the eighteenth and nineteenth centuries. Although severely damaged during the Second World War, the palace and its grounds have now been fully restored.

LEFT: The Marienkirche (St. Mary's Church) is Berlin's oldest structure. Work first began on the church in 1292, although the tower was added in the fifteenth century, and it was renovated in the 1790s. In this view, the church is dwarfed by Berlin's Fernsehturm (Television Tower).

RIGHT: The Schloss Charlottenburg (Charlottenburg Palace) was built as an Electoral retreat, and the sprawling palace and grounds were extended by later Prussian monarchs. The extensive ornamental gardens behind the palace are built around a large lake—the Karpfenteich—and lie on the banks of the River Spree.

LEFT: Friedrich Wilhelm I, Elector of Brandenburg (1620–88), was known as the Großer Kurfürst (Great Elector) thanks to his ability to expand and strengthen his Brandenburger and Prussian dominions in the aftermath of the Thirty Years War. This statue of the Elector stands in the grounds of the Schloss Charlottenburg.

RIGHT: Sans Souci (or Sanssouci), the former summer palace of Frederick "the Great" at Potsdam, was built in the rococo style between 1745 and 1747 and provided the Prussian monarch with a refuge from the pressures of court and army.

LEFT: The Franzözischer Dom (French Cathedral) on the Gendarmenmarkt was built in the first decade of the eighteenth century by Berlin's extensive French Huguenot community. The tower and porticos were added in 1785.

RIGHT: The German statesman Freiherr (Baron) Karl vom Stein (1757–1831) helped pave the way for German unification in the later nineteenth century. He is honored by this statue, erected in front of the Berlin Abgeordnetenhaus (House of Representatives) in the Prussian Landtag (Regional Parliament) building.

FAR RIGHT: The Prussian King Frederick II "the Great" (1712–86), pictured in the aftermath of one of his rare military defeats—the Battle of Kolin, fought against the Austrians in 1757. Although renowned as a soldier king, Frederick also did much to boost cultural and commercial life in his capital.

LEFT: King Frederick II "the Great" of Prussia, shown in discourse with the great French philosopher and writer Voltaire. Voltaire visited the Prussian court in Berlin shortly before Frederick ascended to the throne.

RIGHT: The Quadriga on top of the Brandenburger Tor (Brandenburg Gate) was designed by Johann Schadow in 1793 as a symbol of victory. It was looted by the French in 1806, but reclaimed when the Prussian army entered Paris in 1814. The iron cross was removed by the East Germans, but restored in 1990.

LEFT: The Konzerthaus Berlin (Berlin Concert House) on the Gendarmenmarkt was built by the architect Karl Schinkel in 1821, at which time it was known as the Schauspielhaus (Playhouse). It was built to replace an earlier theater, which was destroyed by fire in 1817. The building was restored in 1984.

RIGHT: The Hungarian composer and great virtuoso pianist Franz Liszt performing at a concert in Berlin. In fact, there is no evidence this happened—it seemed the composer was forced to cancel his two concert tours of the city at short notice in 1840–41, and he never returned to the Prussian capital.

Berlin.

LEFT: During the popular revolution of 1848, riots turned to open rebellion and barricades were erected throughout Berlin. In this print, a red flag flies over a barricade erected towards the eastern end of the Unter den Linden.

RIGHT: The Krolloper (Kroll Opera House) stood on the western side of the Königsplatz (now the Platz der Republik) and was named after a local restaurant owner who funded its construction. This postcard was produced in 1851, the year it first opened its doors. The bombed-out ruins of the building were finally demolished in 1957.

Neue Königl. Oper vorm. Kroll's Etablissement.

LEFT: This engraving by the artist Kirchoff demonstrates that the ideals of the failed Revolution of 1848 appealed to the disaffected liberal middle classes as well as to workers. The tricolor in the engraving was the black, red and gold flag adopted by the German revolutionaries.

RIGHT: Named for the color of its bricks more than for its politics, the Rotes Rathaus (Red Town Hall) was built in the 1860s in an Italian Renaissance style. It served as the seat of East Berlin's administration before reunification and, from 1991, became the town hall of the unified city.

LEFT: Berlin's Siegessäule (Victory Column) was built to commemorate a Prussian victory over Denmark in 1864. However, after further victories over Austria and France, sculptor Friedrich Drake added this 25 foot high statue of "Victoria" clutching the wreath of victory. Berliners have nicknamed her "Goldense" (Golden Lizzie).

RIGHT: In 1891, German aviation pioneer Otto Lilienthal made a successful unpowered flight in a glider launched from the summit of a man-made hill on the outskirts of Berlin. His craft—similar to a modern hang-glider—was improved, and he continued his experiments until his death in a crash in 1896.

FAR RIGHT: Kaiser Wilhelm II pictured during a military ceremony in Berlin in 1889 with his fellow Germanic ruler, the Emperor Franz-Joseph of Austria-Hungary. A quarter of a century later, the alliance between the two monarchs would lead directly to the outbreak of the First World War.

LEFT: At the start of the First World War, women were encouraged to perform jobs which had hitherto been the reserve of men. This lady is a female tram conductor, pictured standing on the steps of a Looman tram or street car.

RIGHT: A female street cleaner in Berlin during the First World War. The demands of the German army meant that women had to take over an increasing range of jobs which were usually performed by men as the war dragged on.

FAR RIGHT: The Museumsinsel (Museum Island) viewed from the north, where the River Spree forms into two channels. The building in the foreground is the Bodemuseum (formerly the Kaiser Friedrich Museum), built in 1904.

LEFT: Designed by renowned architect Ernst von Ihne, The Bode Museum on the northern tip of the Museumsinsel first opened in 1904 as the Kaiser Friedrich Museum. It now houses a priceless collection of sculptures and Byzantine art.

RIGHT: An early zeppelin airship flies over Berlin shortly after the outbreak of the First World War—a morale-boosting display of Imperial German technology. In this view, the airship is shown flying over the Rotes Rathaus (Red Town Hall) and the old Stadttheater (State Theater).

BELOW: The River Havel runs through Potsdam before joining the River Spree at Spandau, in Berlin's north-western suburbs. During the Imperial era, the banks of the Havel were popular with weekend picnickers and boating parties.

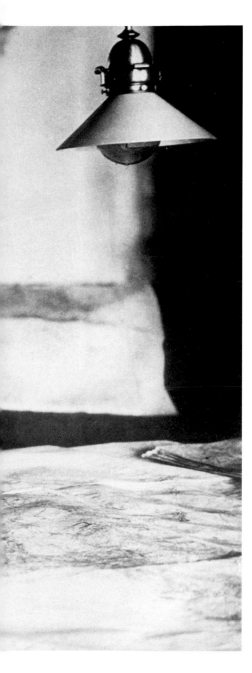

LEFT: Field Marshal von Hindenburg (left), planning strategy with Kaiser Wilhelm II and Field Marshal Ludendorf (right) in the Stadtschloss. Both generals were extremely able commanders, and Berlin was spared the ravages of war partly through their efforts.

RIGHT: The Bezirkswappen (District Coats of Arms) of Berlin's districts reflect the feudal origins of the city—many portray their original function as Hohenzollern hunting parks, or their proximity to electoral or royal palaces.

Neukölln   Tempelhof   Steglitz   Zehlendorf

Wilmersdorf   Charlottenburg   Spandau   Reinickendorf

Wedding   Tiergarten   Kreuzberg   Schöneberg

RIGHT: The River Spree once divided the two medieval settlements of Berlin and Cölln, between which lay an island where the Hohenzollern rulers built their castle—the Stadtschloss. This view of the medieval heart of Berlin is now dominated by the Berliner Dom, facing the reconstructed Nikolaiviertel district on the opposite bank of the river.

RIGHT: The neo-classical Belvedere in the gardens of the Charlottenburg Palace (the Schlossgardten) was built by architect Carl Langhans during the late eighteenth century. It served as a tea room for royal picnickers, although today it is used to house an exhibition of porcelain manufacture.

Imperial Berlin

Imperial Berlin

When Berlin became an Imperial capital in 1871, it embarked upon a period of rapid expansion, developing almost overnight from a sleepy and provincial capital into one of the world's great metropolises.

Most of the economic boost for this was provided by the demands of Berlin industrialists, aided by war reparations gleaned from the French and the Austrians. In Berlin, the decades between 1870 and 1910 were known as the Gründerzeit (The Foundation Years), when the city firmly established itself as one of the great capital cities of Europe, with the civic architecture and economic, social and cultural influence to support its newly acquired status.

This rarely-seen collection of photos from the archives of the Library of Congress show Berlin as it appeared during the last decades of its heyday. While a few of these images date from around 1880, when the expansion of the city was at it height, the majority were taken between 1900 and 1914, when the First World War brought this heyday to a sudden end. Therefore, they show Berlin at the zenith of its Imperial splendor and status—at the very end of the Gründerzeit.

Of course, this collection of photographs makes no attempt to show all aspects of Berlin life during this period. Only a handful of images show the working class majority of the city's population. The squalor, overcrowding and tension of the working districts has been avoided by the photographer, who concentrated his efforts on Berlin's parks, palaces and main thoroughfares—the playground of the German bourgeoisie. However, they still capture something of the mood of the period—a confident, even brash atmosphere when Berlin was a city to be proud of.

This unique collection of images also shows a Berlin which no longer exists. Most of the elegant buildings shown here were badly damaged or destroyed during the Second World War, or were even demolished by post-war urban planners. However, many still survive as museums, civic buildings or tourist attractions, as a new generation of Berliners have found new uses for these magnificent structures. The majority of these grand buildings were first built through royal or Imperial patronage, an architectural reflection of the growing status and power of the Hohenzollern dynasty.

The boom of the late nineteenth century changed the appearance of the city. The surrounding countryside was swallowed up by new developments, and a ring of industrial areas and worker's suburbs was created, fuelled by Berlin's new status as a leading industrial city. The working class tenements—the Mietskasernen (Rent Barracks)—were not particularly photogenic and, therefore, there is no comprehensive photographic record of life within them.

What we are left with is a more prosperous Berlin, a city of genteel cafes and restaurants, lush parks and magnificent museums and galleries. For the bourgeoisie, the Unter den Linden and the center of the city near it was the place to see and be seen. For these Berliners, weekends were spent strolling in Potsdam, or picnicking beside the River Spree. This is the world which was changed forever on August 1, 1914, when the Kaiser announced Germany's declaration of war from the balcony of the Stadtschloss. Four years later he abdicated, and the Imperial edifice crumbled forever.

PREVIOUS PAGE: The Siegessäule (Victory Column) in the Tiergarten, with the Reichstag building in the background, as they looked around 1900. The Reichstag was first opened in 1894.

RIGHT: The Brandenburger Tor (Brandenburg Gate) as it looked immediately before the First World War. It was commissioned as a symbol of peace and built by Carl Gotthard Langhans between 1788 and 1791.

LEFT: Shortly before the First World War, Berlin was a bustling metropolis of four million people and, as this photograph taken in February 1913 shows, the introduction of the automobile caused traffic congestion on the streets of the capital.

RIGHT: The Siegessäule (Victory Column) is one of the premier landmarks in Berlin and was designed by Heinrich Strack to commemorate a Prussian victory over Denmark in 1864. Further victories against the Austrians and the French led to it being surmounted by a bronze sculpture of Victoria, sculpted by Freidrich Drake. Berliners call the statue "Goldelse" (Golden Lizzie).

LEFT: One of the attractions of the royal park at Sanssouci at Potsdam, this windmill was built by order of Frederick "the Great" to provide a rustic ambience to the landscape.

RIGHT: The Altes Museum (Old Museum), pictured before the First World War. This neo-classical building was designed by Karl Schinkel and built during the 1820s.

BELOW: One of the prettiest squares in Berlin, the Gendarmenmarkt is dominated by the Konzerthaus (Concert Hall), built in 1821 by Karl Schinkel, and the early-eighteenth century Französischer Dom (French Cathedral).

BELOW: When this photograph was taken on the eve of the First World War, the Potsdamer Platz (Potsdam Square) was one of the busiest squares in Europe, a major transport hub surrounded by bars and cafes. None of it survived the Second World War.

LEFT: The Staatsoper (Berlin State Opera) on the Unter den Linden was originally the Hofoper (Court Opera House), which was rebuilt after a fire in the 1840s.

RIGHT: An artificial waterfall in Viktoria Park in the Kreuzberg district of Berlin, one of the many green spaces opened to the public before the First World War. In the background is a statue dedicated to the Wars of Liberation against Napoleon (1813–15).

BELOW: The Friedrich-Wilhelms-Universität (Frederick William University) on the Unter den Linden was founded by Wilhelm von Humboldt in 1810 as the University of Berlin. In 1949, it was renamed the Humboldt-Universität (Humboldt University) in honor of its founder.

BELOW: The Reichstag, seat of the German Parliament, as it appeared around 1900. It was constructed between 1884 and 1894, funded by war reparations provided by the French after their defeat in 1870–71.

BELOW: Inspired by Windsor Castle, the neo-Gothic Schloss Babelsberg set amid its own luxurious grounds in Potsdam was built in 1833 as an alternative summer retreat for the royal family. This view was taken shortly before the First World War.

BELOW: The Orangerieschloss (Orangery) in Potsdam was built during the 1850s by orders of King Frederick Wilhelm IV. It was designed as a garden palace and inspired by Italian renaissance architecture.

LEFT: The Marmorpalais (Marble Palace) was built during the late eighteenth century in the grounds of Potsdam's New Garden, on the banks of a lake—the Heiliger See. Before the First World War, it was a favorite retreat of Kaiser Wilhelm II.

LEFT: The most famous landmark in the Potsdam is the large landscaped park of Sanssouci (meaning "without worries"), laid out on the orders of Frederick "the Great".

RIGHT: Frederick "the Great" was attracted to Sanssouci by its fine views, and its proximity to his capital, although it was only one of three royal parks which surrounded the capital.

LEFT: The Unter den Linden (meaning literally "under the lime trees") was the premier boulevard in Berlin. This view is dominated by the equestrian statue of Frederick "the Great".

RIGHT: Queen Louise, the wife of King Frederick Wilhelm III, died in 1810 and her grieving husband erected this memorial in Potsdam's royal park.

LEFT: A general view of Potsdam taken shortly before the First World War. The summer residence of the Hohenzollerns, it was the perfect place to escape the congestion of Berlin.

LEFT: The Brandenburger Tor (Brandenburg Gate) viewed from the Pariserplatz (Paris Square), as it appeared around 1880. It was dominated by the Quadriga, a personification of victory astride a four-horse chariot.

RIGHT: The Victoria Hotel on the Unter den Linden as it looked on the eve of the First World War. It stood on the intersection with Friedrichstrasse, one of the liveliest corners in Berlin during this period.

LEFT: The Royal Yacht Louise, berthed on the River Havel in front of the Matrosenstation (Sailor's Training Station) in Potsdam. The yacht was built in 1897, just a few years before this photograph was taken.

RIGHT: The Royal residence of the Stadtschloss (City Palace) viewed from the Lustgarten (Pleasure Garden) with its granite bowl fountain. The attractive gardens were laid out on the banks of the River Spree but they had become a venue for military parades by 1900.

LEFT: The Goethe Memorial in the Tiergarten Park was carved in marble by sculptor Fritz Schapel and erected in 1880. The figures around its base represent lyric, poetry, drama and science.

RIGHT: The Neue Wache (New Guardhouse) on the eastern Unter den Linden was designed by Karl Schinkel, and constructed in 1816–18 as the headquarters of the Royal Guard.

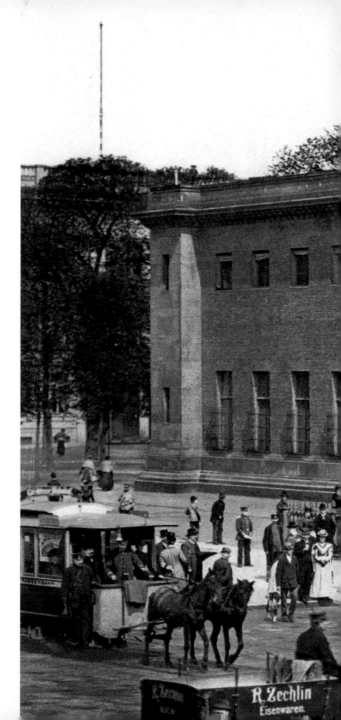

LEFT: The Baroque Zughaus (Old Arsenal) is the oldest structure on the Unter den Linden and was completed in 1706. In 1875, the building was turned into a military museum and today houses the Deutsches Historisches Museum (German Historical Museum).

BELOW: The Kaiser Wilhelmsbrücke (Kaiser Wilhelm Bridge) over the River Spree connected the Kaiser-Wilhelm Straße on the eastern bank to the Unter den Linden on the far side of what is now the Museumsinsel. The bridge was destroyed by German troops in April 1945.

LEFT: The Unter den Linden, viewed from the Schlossbrücke (Castle Bridge), looking west, as it looked immediately before the First World War. The building on the left is the Zughaus (Old Arsenal).

LEFT: The Kaiser-Wilhelm-Gedächtniskirche (Emperor Wilhelm's Memorial Church) on the Kürfurstendamm was built in the 1890s by distinguished architect Frans Schwechten. The project was ordered by Kaiser Wilhelm II in honor of his father.

RIGHT: The Kaiser Friedrich Mausoleum was erected beside the Friedenskirche (Church of Peace) in Potsdam in the royal park of Sanssouci. The marble sarcophagus was designed by sculptor Reinhold Begas.

LEFT: Glienicker Brücke (Glienicke Bridge) spans the Havel River, linking Potsdam to Berlin. In this early twentieth century photograph, it is viewed from the nearby Babelsberg.

RIGHT: The Neptunbrunnen (Neptune Fountain), sculpted by Reinhold Begas in 1888, was first erected outside the Stadtschloss (City Palace) but has since been moved to the Alexanderplatz.

LEFT: The Nationaldenkmal (National Memorial), dedicated to the memory of Kaiser Wilhelm I in 1889, once stood facing the Stadtschloss on the banks of the Spree Canal. It was subsequently demolished.

LEFT: The Friedrichsbrücke (Frederick's Bridge) spanning the River Spree was built in the late eighteenth century to link Berlin and Cölln. In this view from around 1900, the Alte Nationalgalerie (Old National Gallery) can be seen in the background.

RIGHT: The Hallesches Tor Station, with the Belle Alliance Platz (now the Mehringplatz) beyond, viewed from the Mehringbrücke shortly before the First World War. This same view, featuring the Victory Column designed by Christian Rauch, was also painted by the great German impressionist Ernst Kirschner in 1914.

LEFT: Café Bauer on the Unter den Linden lay on its intersection with the Friedrichstrasse, and consequently was a bustling venue before the First World War. The café itself was destroyed during the Second World War.

RIGHT: The equestrian statue of Frederick "the Great" on the Unter den Linden was erected by Christian Rauch in 1851, having taken the sculptor two decades to complete. Around the base of its plinth are depictions of all of Frederick's senior generals.

115

LEFT: A household on the move through the streets of Berlin in a photograph taken some time around 1900. During this period, conditions for Berlin's skilled workers were still hard, and there was no social safety net if a family fell on hard times.

RIGHT: A Berlin laborer enjoying a lunch of soup and coffee supplied by his spouse. Such scenes would have been commonplace in the decades before the First World War.

Weimar Berlin and the Hitler Years

Weimar Berlin and the Hitler Years

Germans claimed some sort of victory from the First World War in that the "fatherland" had been spared the ravages of war. On August 9, the Kaiser abdicated and went into exile, ending a Hohenzollern rule over Berlin which had lasted for more than five centuries. Two days later, the war came to an end. By that stage Berlin was already in turmoil. During the last months of the conflict, the workers in Berlin's factories had staged anti-war strikes, while demonstrations had been put down by German troops. As the war ended a new conflict began, fought on the streets of Berlin between supporters of left and right. Martial law was imposed by the leaders of the new Weimar Republic; the violence only came to an end when the communists were murdered by right-wing paramilitaries and their supporters defeated in a series of bloody clashes.

This was the blood-soaked dawn of the Weimar Republic, a period in German history known as much for its blossoming of culture and hedonistic exuberance as for its political instability. In many ways, this was a Golden Age for Berlin, when the city attracted some of the best and most innovative artists, playwrights, sculptors, architects and film producers in the world. This was the era of Bauhaus, of Bertold Brecht and the expressionist painter Ernst Kirchner. Berlin was a swinging place, and even the economic crash of 1923 and the poverty which resulted failed to dampen the exuberant mood of Weimar Berlin.

However, the economic climate encouraged the growth of political extremism and, by 1932, the NSDAP ("Nazi" Party) had become the largest single party in the Reichstag despite their continued lack of popularity in Berlin, where the majority of the population voted Communist. The burning of the Reichstag early the following year marked a watershed—Hitler used the fire to set aside the constitution and call another election. This time the left was muzzled, and Hitler consequently swept to power. By 1934, he was the leader of a one-party state. What followed were book burnings, the victimization and then imprisonment of Berlin's Jewish population, and the attempted rebuilding of "Red Berlin" in the Nazi mould. The Olympics of 1936 gave the Nazis the opportunity to show their "purged" city to the world, a city where Jews, "undesirables" or political opponents were removed to concentration camps.

The outbreak of war in 1939 had little immediate effect on Berlin, although perhaps it did spare the city the worst excesses of Nazi urban planning—the grandiose visions for the city developed by Nazi architect Albert Speer were set aside in order to concentrate on the war effort. By 1943 it was clear that Berlin was at risk and a mass evacuation was ordered. The first wave of bombs fell in November 1943 and, within months, much of the city centre had been destroyed and many of Berlin's most famous landmarks lay in ruins. However, worse was to come for the city. A mass bombing in February 1945 was followed two months later by an assault by the Soviet army. After almost two weeks of bitter and costly street fighting, the Soviets captured the ruined city, forcing Hitler to commit suicide as Soviet troops approached his bunker refuge. The war was over, but Berlin was a broken city. It would soon become a divided one.

PREVIOUS PAGE: The Universität zu Berlin (University of Berlin) was founded in 1810 by reformer and philosopher Wilhelm von Humbolt, and it was its libraries which were purged by the Nazis when they staged their mass book burning in May 1933. In 1946, the university was renamed after its founder.

RIGHT: The Pergamon Museum on the Museumsinsel was built between 1910 and 1930 to house full-sized reconstructions of Ancient Greek or Persian monuments, including the Pergamon Altar and the Marketplace of Melitus. The museum also houses a significant collection of artifacts from the ancient world.

LEFT: A recruiting poster for the Küntzel Guard Cavalry Schützen Detachment of the Freikorps (Free Corps), drawn by Ernst Janetzke in 1918. This paramilitary formation was responsible for hunting down communist leader Rosa Luxemburg.

RIGHT: This photograph, taken on January 3, 1919 shows revolutionary German soldiers driving through the Brandenburger Tor (Brandenburg Gate). The Kaiser had been forced to abdicate when soldiers of the German Imperial Guard sided with the anti-war revolutionaries.

LEFT: A political rally, organised by the Communist Spartakusbund (Spartikist League), in late 1918. The German Revolution which led to the overthrow of the Kaiser was brutally crushed by paramilitary troops, acting on the orders of the Social Democratic Weimar government.

RIGHT: "Your Fatherland is in danger—enlist!" A Freikorps recruiting poster, produced in Berlin during 1918. The Freikorps were recruited to crush the German Revolution of 1918–19.

LEFT: German troops returning from the battlefields of the First World War march through the streets of Berlin in December 1918. Their only victory was that Germany had been spared the ravages of war.

RIGHT: During the First World War, the Allied naval blockade of Germany led to widespread shortages and food was in short supply so sections of parks and boulevards were turned over to Berliners to grow vegetables. In this photograph, taken in early 1919, women are shown digging a new plot on the side of a city street.

LEFT: Former German soldiers and paramilitary troops (Freikorps) fought revolutionaries on the streets of Berlin during 1919. In this photograph taken that December, these soldiers are supported by a makeshift armored car.

ABOVE: A well-armed truck filled with right-wing Freikorps troops, captured by a photographer as it patrolled through Potzdamerplatz in April 1920. The previous month, the Weimar government was temporarily ousted in a right-wing coup, but lack of popular support meant that the putsch failed.

RIGHT: Rosa Luxembourg (1871–1919), the Polish-born co-founder of the Spartakusbund (Sparrikist League), a communist revolutionary movement which attracted widespread support in the aftermath of the First World War. She and her fellow communist leader Karl Liebknecht were murdered by right-wing Freikorps troops in January 1919.

LEFT: German troops, carrying the old Imperial Reichkriegsflagge (War Ensign) which was formally abolished in 1919, but which remained in use until 1921. The photograph was taken in front of the Adlon Hotel on the Unter den Linden in April 1920, in the aftermath of a failed right-wing coup.

RIGHT: In the aftermath of the German Revolution of 1918–19, police, paramilitary groups and the German army continued to maintain an armed presence on the streets of Berlin. This photograph, taken in November 1920, shows a light machine gun team protecting the Stadtschloss.

LEFT: Following a street battle in November 1920, right-wing Freikorps troops occupy a barricade erected by the communists. Scenes of this kind were commonplace during the years following the end of the First World War.

RIGHT: In July 1922, a new radio station opened up in Berlin, capable of sending and receiving messages across the Atlantic. The Weimar years were marked by great technological, social, and cultural progress, as well as by economic disaster and political instability.

LEFT: A 1,000 mark note, printed during the Weimar Republic. In 1923, the German economy collapsed and paper money of this kind became virtually worthless. That December, the exchange rate had become so bad that one US dollar was worth 4.2 billion marks.

RIGHT: In 1923, a combination of world depression and heavy war reparations led to great inflation where the German economy collapsed virtually overnight. This Berlin woman is shown lighting her stove using a pile of otherwise worthless bank notes.

LEFT: During the Great Inflation of 1923, German banknotes were rendered worthless. In this photograph taken in Berlin during the early years of the Weimar Republic, workers are collecting bank notes into bales of waste paper.

RIGHT: As a result of the Great Inflation of 1923, many Berliners were rendered destitute, and unemployment reached record levels. This poverty-stricken family were captured by a photographer during the mid 1920s.

LEFT: In 1924, the American sprint champion Loren Murchison was beaten by Hubert Houben in a 100 meter race held in Berlin. Houben was duly hailed a hero by the Berliners.

RIGHT: During the Weimar years, this group of young women demonstrate their equality by dressing in male clothing and smoking cigars. However, few of them seem to be enjoying the experience. The photograph was taken in a Berlin smoking club in early 1927.

LEFT: The great German Jewish physicist Albert Einstein, photographed while addressing a meeting of fellow scientists in Berlin in 1929. Einstein served as a Director of Berlin's Kaiser Wilhelm Institute of Physics until he was forced to flee Germany in 1933.

RIGHT: These two election posters were used by the Social Democrats in Berlin during the election of 1930. Both urge voters not to support the communists, as that would simply allow the Nazi Party to gain power by weakening the left-wing vote.

LEFT: Berlin's Potsdamer Platz, photographed in 1930 at the height of the Weimar era. At time the effects of the Great Inflation had resulted in one in four of the city's population being out of work, and political unrest was widespread.

ABOVE: Before the First World War, the Lustgarten in front of the Stadtschloss was occasionally used to hold military parades. During the 1930s, the Nazis transformed it into a site for mass party rallies.

LEFT: On the streets outside the Berliner Dom (Berlin Cathedral), posters urge voters to support the joint candidacy of Field Marshal Hindenburg and Adolf Hitler. The election of March 1933 was a victory for the Nazis, although the majority of Berliners preferred to support the communists.

RIGHT: In April 1933, the Nazis called for a boycott of Jewish shops, an initiative which was reinforced by squads of paramilitary Sturmabteilung (SA) "brownshirts", who began openly attacking Jews on the streets of Berlin.

LEFT: A group of German university students are among the first of the city's population to visit Berlin's Gas Protection School, which opened in 1933. It opened within months of Hitler being named Chancellor.

RIGHT: In May 1933, the Nazis staged a mass burning of "decadent" books in the Opernplatz (now the Bebelplatz), opposite the Berlin University. Some 20,000 books were consigned to the flames in this wanton orgy of destruction. "Decadent" authors included Thomas Mann, Bertold Brecht, Ernest Hemingway and H.G. Wells.

LEFT: Hitler's motorcade, photographed as it progressed through the Brandenburger Tor (Brandenburg Gate) and on down the Unter den Linden in December 1933. The occasion for the ceremony was the opening of the Prussian Bundesrat (Council of State).

RIGHT: German boxer Max Schmeling is greeted by crowds at Berlin Airport in 1936. The former World Heavyweight Champion had just defeated Joe Louis in New York and his victory was turned into a propaganda coup by the Nazis. Louis defeated Schmeling in a rematch two years later.

LEFT: The Olympiastadion (Olympic Stadium) was built for the Olympic Games of 1936 and was subsequently used as a Nazi sports ground, and as a venue to hold Nazi rallies. After the war, it was maintained by the British. In this view of the stadium taken in 1981, its appearance has changed little since it was first opened. It has subsequently been refurbished.

ABOVE: During the preparations for the 1936 Olympic Games, Hitler ordered that the lime trees on the Unter den Linden be chopped down and replaced by these Festschmuck (Festive Decorations) celebrating the Third Reich. The trees were replanted after the war.

LEFT: For the 1936 Olympic Games, Berlin was transformed into something akin to a Nazi stageset. Here the Olympic torch is seen being brought into the Lustgarten in front of the Stadtschloss, where the Olympic flame was ignited in front of a crowd of athletes and dignitaries.

ABOVE: A 12 pfennig stamp, launched to commemorate the Berlin Olympic Games of 1936. Hitler hoped the games would serve as a showcase for the city, and for his Third Reich, and so considerable effort was put in to turning the event into a propaganda vehicle.

RIGHT: The airship *Hindenburg* (LZ-129) is pictured flying over the Olympiastadion (Olympic Stadium) during the Olympic Games, held in Berlin in 1936. Hitler used the games as a propaganda vehicle for Nazi Germany, and the brand-new airship made an impressive spectacle as it flew over the city.

LEFT: The celebrated American athlete Jesse Owens, pictured at the 1936 Olympics. Victory by this decidedly non-Aryan runner was something of a setback for the Nazi propaganda machine.

RIGHT: After the rise to power of the Nazis, shops and businesses owned by Jewish proprietors were targeted by Nazi agitators. This shop was damaged and ransacked during the Kristallnacht riots of November 1937.

LEFT: German schoolgirls clutching Nazi flags greet Hitler as he drives in state along the Wilhelmstrasse in September 1938. The photograph was taken on the Wilhelmplatz, which was renamed the Thälmannplatz in 1950.

RIGHT: After returning from the Munich Conference in October 1938, Hitler was greeted at Berlin's Anhalter railway station by cheering crowds who believed he had guaranteed peace for Germany. In this photograph, he is shown receiving a bouquet of flowers from two small girls, while Field Marshall Goering and Propaganda Minister Goebbels watch with approval.

167

LEFT: The ruins of the Brandenburger Tor (Brandenburg Gate) as it looked in the immediate aftermath of the Fall of Berlin, 1945. The Reichstag and the area around the Brandenburger Tor were captured by Soviet troops on April 30.

RIGHT: A Soviet SU-152 Self-Propelled Gun on the streets of Berlin during the final assault on the city in late April 1945. The defiant graffiti reads "Berlin remains German".

LEFT: A Soviet soldier raising the Soviet flag over the smoking ruins of the Reichstag. This iconic photograph was staged for the benefit of army photographer Yevgeny Khaldei. When the flag was first raised at 10.00 pm on April 30, by Sergeant Minin there was no photographer there to record the event.

RIGHT: A Soviet woman soldier, captured by army photographer Yevgeny Khaldei while directing military convoys through the rubble of Berlin. The sign behind her proclaims the date—May 1, 1945—by which stage all but the last few pockets of German resistance had been crushed.

LEFT: In this staged photograph taken by army photographer Yevgeny Khaldei, victorious Soviet troops contemplate the burnt ruins of Berlin—"the Fascist Lair". The last German troops surrendered on May 2, 1945. The ruins of the Kaiser Wilhelm Gedächtniskirche (Kaiser William Memorial Church) can be seen in the distance.

RIGHT: In another photograph staged by army photographer Yevgeny Khaldei, Soviet troops are shown storming the burnt-out remains of the Reichstag. Despite being in ruins since the fire of 1933, the building remained a symbol of German nationalism, and therefore became a key objective during the Battle for Berlin in April–May 1945.

LEFT: A column of Soviet 76.2mm anti-tank guns and their crews guard a square in central Berlin as fires still ravage the buildings in the background. The photograph was probably taken by Soviet army photographer Dmitri Balermants on May 2, 1945.

BELOW: The view from the roof of the Reichstag on May 2, 1945—the day the last of the city's defenders surrendered to the Soviet army. When the guns fell silent the city lay in ruins.

LEFT: A young female Soviet soldier directs military traffic in the center of Berlin, while battle-damaged buildings still blaze fiercely behind her. The photograph was taken by Soviet army photographer Dmitri Balermants before the surrender of the last pockets of German resistance on May 2, 1945.

ABOVE: A Soviet T34/76 tank, one of thousands that participated in the assault on Berlin in April 1945. It now forms part of the Soviet War Memorial in the Tiergarten.

LEFT: The Judischer Friedhof (Jewish Cemetery) in Weissensee, in the north-eastern suburbs of the city. It was laid out by architect Hugo Lift in 1878 and somehow survived the Holocaust. Today, it is one of the few surviving reminders of Berlin's vibrant pre-war Jewish community.

LEFT: The Kaiser Wilhelm Gedächtniskirche (Kaiser Wilhelm Memorial Church) on the Kurfürstendamm was built during the 1890s to commemorate the grandfather of the last Kaiser. It was virtually destroyed during a bombing raid in early 1943, and all that now remains of the original church is the ruined remains of its tower.

BELOW: The Olympiastadion (Olympic Stadium) in Berlin was built in 1934–36 to house the 1936 Olympic Games. It was later used for massed Nazi rallies. After the war it remained somewhat dilapidated until 2000, when the stadium was renovated.

RIGHT: Over six million of Europe's Jewish population died during the Holocaust, including the overwhelming majority of Berlin's 160,000 strong pre-war Jewish community. Six decades after the end of the Second World War, this Holocaust Denkmal was finally unveiled in the center of Berlin in their memory.

Cold War Berlin

Cold War Berlin

When the Second World War ended in May 1948, Berlin was little more than a smoking ruin. Some 250,000 civilians had died during the war, including most of the city's 160,000-strong Jewish community. When he returned to Berlin in 1948, playwright Bertold Brecht said that the city was little more than "a pile of rubble next to Potsdam." Houses lay in ruins, there was no water or power, and bodies still lay amid the rubble. Clearing the debris took years and, in the process, the landscape of the city was altered, as mountains of rubble were created. One of these—the Teufelsberg—still exists today.

Like the rest of Germany, Berlin was divided into four zones of occupation, controlled by the British, French, Americans and Soviets. In theory, the city was administered by a joint Allied command, but tensions soon rose between the Soviets and the three Western powers. In 1946, a new city government was elected, but the Soviets refused to recognize the pro-Western administration. These tensions soon developed into what was dubbed "The Cold War" and, in June 1948, the Soviets cut all road links between Berlin and the Western zones of Germany. The Western Allies responded by staging the Berlin Airlift, where supplies were flown into the city. In October 1949, the Soviet Zone became part of the German Democratic Republic (GDR), a response to the formation of the Federal Republic of Germany in the west. In theory Berlin was still a unified whole—in practice it was devolving into two cities.

By the 1950s, West Berlin had become the "Last Outpost of the Free World"—a bastion of Western political and economic systems in the midst of Communist Eastern Europe. As Berlin became the spy capital of Europe, both East and West continued to mould their parts of the city in their own way. In West Berlin, the inhabitants benefited from American economic aids and recovery from the war was significantly faster than in the East. This was exacerbated by East German urban planning—"decadent" old landmarks such as the Stadtschloss were demolished, and new roads and buildings erected which better reflected the Germany envisioned by the leaders of the GDR. Then on August 13, 1961 the East Germans ringed West Berlin with wire—a temporary barrier which was soon replaced by a permanent wall. Berlin had now become a divided city.

For the next 29 years, the Berlin Wall remained a symbol of the Cold War. Within weeks it led to a visit to West Berlin by President Kennedy, who famously declared his support for the Berliners. During the 1960s, the two cities continued to develop separately—new museums, galleries and cultural building were built in the Tiergarten to replace those lost to East Berlin, while in the East the ravages of urban planning led to the remodeling of Alexanderplatz and the historic heart of the city. East Germany's secret police—the Stasi—monitored the lives of East Berliners, while the residents of in the West Berlin continued to rely on subsidies, a situation which led to political friction between Berliners and other West Germans.

However, times were changing. Following the advent of "Perestroika" in the Soviet Union, the leaders of the GDR became increasingly unable to control their population. Celebrations of the fortieth anniversary of the East German state were followed within days by the ousting of its communist leader. On November 9, 1989, the checkpoints on the Berlin Wall were opened and thousands of East Berliners surged across the border. The Cold War had officially come to an end. As protesters set about the wall with hammers and pickaxes, Berliners celebrated the reunification of their city.

PREVIOUS PAGE: In 1945, the victorious Soviets erected this Soviet War Memorial in the Tiergarten, just a short distance from the Brandenburger Tor (Brandenburg Gate) and the Reichstag. It has been estimated that over 80,000 Soviet soldiers died during the Fall of Berlin in 1945.

RIGHT: A mother cooks for her children in the street in the aftermath of the Second World War. Tens of thousands of Berliners were made homeless by the war, and feeding and housing the civilian population became one of the most important tasks facing the military quadrumvirate who now governed the city.

LEFT: A Soviet soldier poses with a manikin amid the rubble of a Berlin street in 1945. The Soviet Union had endured untold hardships during the war and, consequently, the Soviet forces regarded themselves first and foremost as an army of occupation, and its soldiers treated the Berliners accordingly.

RIGHT: In the months following the end of the Second World War, Berliners tried to come to terms with the destruction and partition of their city, and of the bloodbath which brought about the end of the Third Reich. In this street scene, photographed in late-1945, the bench still bears the inscription "Nicht für Juden (Not for Jews)".

LEFT: The ruins of Berlin's Anhalter Station near the Potsdamer Platz, photographed in July 1945. Before the war it was the city's largest railroad station, the "Gateway to the South"—the terminus for trains from Spain, Italy, Austria, Czechoslovakia, and Southern Germany. Today, only the S-Bahn station remains of this once great railroad terminal.

RIGHT: Berliners attempted to get on with their lives as best they could after the war. In this rare color photograph taken on the Potsdamer Strasse in July 1945, civilians queue for a battered bus amid the ruins of their city.

LEFT: When the war ended, Berliners were forced to sell what few goods they still had in an effort to survive. Consequently the Black Market flourished with great demand for cheap cameras, watches and antiques. In this photograph taken in July 1945, Soviet and American soldiers show an interest in goods offered by a civilian.

RIGHT: Sergeant Marino of the US 2nd Armored Division, was one of the first American soldiers to enter Berlin after the partition of the city into four military zones. In this photograph, taken in July 1945, he is shown sitting on top of a Sherman tank, somewhere in the southern area of the city.

LEFT: The damaged remains of a German 88mm flak gun stands in front of the ruins of the Kaiser Wilhelm Gedächtniskirche (Kaiser Wilhelm Memorial Church) on the Kurfürstendamm in 1946. When German playwright Bertolt Brecht visited the city two years later he described it as "a pile of rubble next to Potsdam."

RIGHT: In the years following the end of the war, teams of laborers—many of them women—worked to clear the streets of rubble and to prepare bricks for reuse in the rebuilding of the city. This photograph was taken in August 1946.

LEFT: Two children walk home from school through a landscape of shattered buildings, in a photograph taken in October 1947. Both are carrying army mess tins as the military authorities ensured that hot meals were served to the children at lunchtimes.

RIGHT: In December 1947, Soviet Engineers blew up the remains of Hitler's bunker in the grounds of the Reichskanzlei (State Chancellery), which can be seen in the background of this photograph. The conical structure is the remains of the bunker's main air vent.

LEFT: Women workers carry a section of rail, in a photograph taken in March 1948, during work to restore Berlin's transport infrastructure. In the background can be seen the remains of a bombed-out factory in the American zone of the city.

LEFT: American C-47 transport planes are unloaded at Berlin's Tempelhof Airport in June 1948, at the start of the Berlin Airlift. A mixture of British and American aircraft were used in this operation, and "Operation Vittles" proved a resounding success.

RIGHT: In this staged photograph taken in July 1948, children and adults watch from the rooftop of a war-ravaged building as American transport planes fly vital supplies into the city during the Berlin Airlift.

LEFT: During the Soviet blockade of Berlin in 1948–49, German police under Soviet control inspect a truck attempting to enter the British sector of Berlin along the Unter den Linden in November 1948. The Brandenburger Tor (Brandenburg Gate) can be seen in the background.

RIGHT: For several years after the end of the war, Berliners were forced to live as best they could amid the ruins of their homes. This view of a once fashionable street in the American sector was taken in the winter of 1948, and shows the devastation which surrounded Berliners for years after the end of the war.

LEFT: A group of schoolgirls in West Berlin on their way home from school peer into the window of a food shop in late 1948. At that time, all food was flown into Berlin on board Allied aircraft and luxury foods such as confectionery and sweets were virtually unobtainable.

RIGHT: While most supplies brought in during the Berlin Airlift were transported by the U.S. Air Force, a significant proportion was flown into the city on board British planes such as this C-47 of the Royal Air Force, photographed during its approach to Tempelhof Airport in late 1948.

LEFT: On the eve of Christmas 1948, American transport planes brought Santa Claus to Berlin, laden with presents for the children of West Berlin, in a propaganda exercise staged by the US military administration. Despite the blockade of the city, the lifeline of the Berlin Airlift meant that some semblance of normal life could continue for the city's civilian population.

ABOVE: During the Berlin Airlift (1948–49), Allied transport planes flew over 250,000 flights into the city. By the time this photograph was taken on May 11, 1949, when the last flight took place, the Western powers had ably demonstrated their commitment to retain control of their sectors of Berlin.

RIGHT: On May 5, 1949, the Soviet Government announced that it would lift the blockade of Berlin within a week. Two days later, these Berliners can be seen cheering one of the last Allied transport planes to fly into Tempelhof Airfield as part of "Operation Vittles".

LEFT: A crowd of Berliners, photographed on the Kurfürstendamm in February 1955, celebrating the departure of the Soviet Premier Georgi Menenkov. It was felt at the time that conditions could only improve. They were wrong—within six years, the Berlin Wall would divide their city in two.

RIGHT: On August 18, 1961, East German construction workers were photographed building a section of the Berlin Wall by the Potsdamer Platz while East German border guards stood watch. Work started during the previous evening and, by the end of the day, the concrete block wall was more than five feet high.

LEFT: A West Berlin family hold up their two babies so that their grandparents on the far side of the wall can see them. This photograph was taken in late August 1961, just days after the wall was first built. Within a few months the wall would be raised, preventing communication of this kind from taking place.

RIGHT: A street sign pointing nowhere—in August 1961, the northern end of the Charlottenstrasse above its junction with Kochstrasse was sealed off overnight following the construction of the Berlin Wall. The nearest passage through the wall was through Checkpoint Charlie, a few yards to the west.

LEFT: An East German soldier carrying a PPSh sub-machine gun stands guard over the makeshift barrier which was first erected on the night of August 12–13, 1961. Photographed in Potsdamer Platz the following day, the soldier seems impervious to the anger of the crowd of West Berliners on the far side of the wire.

RIGHT: A West Berliner uses his bubble car as a makeshift platform as he waves to friends or relatives on the opposite side of the newly-erected Berlin Wall in September 1961. The speed of the construction took most Berliners by surprise, with families and communities being irrevocably separated.

LEFT: In October 1961, two months after the Berlin Wall was first erected, American and Soviet tanks armed with live ammunition faced each other at Checkpoint Charlie with orders to fire if they were fired upon. After 24 hours, both President Kennedy and Premier Khrushchev agreed to withdraw their troops.

RIGHT: The construction of the Berlin Wall in 1961 meant that the Unter den Linden was sealed off at the Brandenburger Tor (Brandenburg Gate), and the Charlottenburger Chaussee (renamed the Strasse des 17 Juni in 1953) became a dead end. This road—one of Europe's great thoroughfares—would remain divided for another 28 years.

BELOW: The Glieneckerbrücke (Glienecke Bridge) was built in 1907 to span the River Havel, linking Potsdam and Berlin. During the Cold War, it lay on the eastern border of West Berlin and was used as a location for the exchange of captured intelligence agents. The press dubbed it "the Bridge of Spies".

LEFT: A symbol of a divided Berlin, the Brandenburger Tor (Brandenburg Gate) stands behind coils of barbed wire. The photograph was taken in November 1961, two months after the city was divided. Ironically, this wire was erected by the British during the rising East-West tension which followed the building of the wall.

RIGHT: The visit to Berlin by President John F. Kennedy in late July 1963 was a response to the building of the Berlin Wall. His aim was to show that the Western powers were prepared to stand by West Berlin, whatever the actions of the East German and Soviet governments.

LEFT: On July 26, 1963, US President John F. Kennedy addressed the citizens of Berlin in front of the Schoeneberg Rathaus (Town Hall), which had become the new seat of the West Berlin civic authorities. It was there that he made his famous speech which declared the West's solidarity with the city's population, declaring "Ich bin ein Berliner (I am a Berliner)".

RIGHT: In August 1963, an East German teenager called Wolfgang Engels commandeered an armored car and attempted to ram his way through the Berlin Wall. He was shot and captured in the attempt. This photograph shows the aftermath as East German soldiers repair the damage.

LEFT: During the mid 1960s, a young West Berlin couple talk to friends or relatives in an East Berlin apartment building on the far side of the Berlin Wall. The East Berlin authorities frowned on exchanges of this kind, and the Eastern participants risked arrest by the Stasi.

RIGHT: Checkpoint Charlie on the Friedrichstrasse, photographed at the height of the Cold War in August 1966. The checkpoint became a symbol of the Cold War, until it was finally dismantled in 1990.

LEFT: A military ceremony, held on the steps of the Neue Wache (New Guardhouse) on the Unter den Linden in October 1981, to celebrate the 32nd anniversary of the foundation of the German Democratic Republic (GDR). Within nine years the GDR would be no more, replaced by a reunified Germany.

ABOVE: Banknotes produced by the German Democratic Republic (GDR). Despite being one of the more successful of the Warsaw Pact nations, East Germany was unable to match the post-war economic resurgence of its Western counterpart.

RIGHT: In June 1982, U.S. President Ronald Regan visited Berlin in an attempt to put additional pressure on the East German and Soviet governments. Here he is shown standing in front of Checkpoint Charlie, the crossing point in the Berlin Wall which served as a symbol of the Cold War.

LEFT: After the Second World War, Berlin was divided into four zones, each controlled by one of the major Allied powers (Britain, France, America and Russia). The last of these occupying powers finally left the city in 1994, although this array of flags at Checkpoint Charlie serves as a reminder of the manner in which post-war Berlin was divided.

RIGHT: The emblem of the old German Democratic Republic still adorns a building in former East Berlin. The coat of arms shows a hammer and compass in a ring of rye, symbolizing industry, education and agriculture.

FAR RIGHT: The Berlin Wall divided streets—one side finding itself separated from the other—and even cemeteries and parks. Today, only a few small stretches remain, a testimony to the tensions and rivalries of the Cold War.

LEFT: Until 1989, the Kurfürstendamm (or Ku'damm) was the premier shopping street in West Berlin. Named after the Brandenburg Kurfürst (Elector), the boulevard was first laid out in the seventeenth century to connect the Stadtschloss to the hunting grounds of the Grunewald. These buildings date from the eighteenth or early nineteenth centuries.

RIGHT: Karl Marks and Friedrich Engels—the founders of communism—as portrayed in a joint statue. It was cast in 1986, just three years before the fall of the Berlin Wall and now stands in the Marx-Engels Forum, in the heart of former East Berlin.

LEFT: The Fernsehturm (Television Tower) was built as a symbol of progress within East Germany during the 1960s, and the 1,200 foot (365 meter) high tower surmounted by a ball and spike was designed to be visible from everywhere in the city—including all of West Berlin. After reunification, it was adopted as an iconic symbol of the unified city.

RIGHT: The former seat of the East German government was the Staatsratsgebäude (State Council Building), built in 1963 on the Museumsinsel. The GDR authorities decorated this otherwise modern building in a way that attempted to reflect the historic nature of the site on which it was built. In 2006 the building became a Business School.

Reunified Berlin

BELOW: The modern skyline of eastern Berlin, seen from the Strasse des 17 Juni and the Tiergarten. The skyline of the city is dominated by the Fernsehturm (Television Tower), built in the late 1960s by the GDR. On the left is the new Reichstag.

Reunified Berlin

Just as it had come to symbolize the Cold War, the reunited Berlin quickly came to symbolize a new Germany and a unified Europe. The first free elections were held in East Berlin in March 1990 and, four months later, the economies of East and West Germany were combined into one. Finally on October 3, 1990 came the official reunification of Germany. While reunification came at a high economic price for the prosperous West German government, it meant that the business of welding Berlin back into one integrated city could finally begin in earnest.

This process was a difficult one—the restructuring of jobs and industry in Eastern Berlin led to huge resentment, as did the boost reunification gave to the city's property market. Similarly the inhabitants of former West Berlin lost their subsidies and tax perks, and Berliners of both sides of the old border were forced to live in a city where market forces were no longer shaped by political ideals. However, the city received a significant boost in 1991, when the decision was made to move the German capital from Bonn to Berlin. As a result a new wave of state investment helped to speed the process of urban reunification—transport systems were overhauled or replaced, civic buildings were remodeled or rebuilt, and housing was improved throughout the city.

During the 1990s, the regeneration of former East Berlin led to the opening of new shops, bars, restaurants and businesses, and gradually the social heart of the city moved back to where it had always been—in the area between the Unter den Linden and Alexanderplatz. Consequently formerly up-market districts of West Berlin became less desirable. Reunification also meant that former West Berliners could now move into the suburbs around Potsdam and Brandenberg, and therefore the decade was marked by a new wave of suburban development.

The main symbol of this reunified city became the Reichstag, which was remodeled by innovative architect Sir Norman Foster, who saw the building as "a dialogue between old and new". A glass dome was added as a modern version of the old cupola which dominated the original building, but this modern Reichstag has become an architectural expression of unity and democracy, rather than a revisiting of pre-war nationalism. As a seat of the German parliament from 1999 onwards, it witnessed the birth of the "Berlin Republic"—a new and vibrant Germany which looks to the future rather than the past.

In 2001, Mayor Wowereit oversaw the merging of several Berlin districts into new boroughs which spanned the old east-west divide. Then, in November 2005, Berlin saw the election of the first woman and former East German as Chancellor and, whatever political views might be involved, this demonstrated how far Germany had come since the fall of the Berlin Wall just 16 years before. Today, Berlin is a city which is still evolving. Many old Berliners have moved out, while fresh incomers have been attracted to the city. It may have its economic difficulties, and old tensions have not completely gone away, but Berlin still remains one of the most dynamic cities in Europe—a place where the successes and pitfalls of the new "Berlin Republic" have a direct impact on the city's evolving population.

RIGHT: On the evening of October 3, 1990 crowds gathered in front of the Reichstag and the Brandenburger Tor (Brandenburg Gate) to celebrate the reunification of Germany. After 28 years of division, Berlin was finally unified into one city again.

LEFT: The Fall of the Berlin Wall. This photograph was taken on November 10, 1989, between the Potsdamer Platz and the Brandenburger Tor (Brandenburg Gate). The crossing points had opened the previous day and already the wall had become a playground for jubilant Berliners from both East and West.

BELOW: East German soldiers are presented with bouquets of flowers by the crowd, while protesters demolish a section of the Berlin Wall behind them on November 12, 1989, just three days after the border crossings were opened.

LEFT: Berliners celebrate the New Year of 1990 in front of the Brandenburger Tor (Brandenburg Gate), the first New Year celebration since the opening of the East German borders just over two months before. Within a year, the two German states would be reunited.

BELOW: The original Reichstag, built in 1884-94, was badly damaged by fire in 1933 but, after the reunification of Germany, it was decided to restore the building and to make it the seat of the German parliament.

LEFT: The original plans, drawn up by Sir Norman Foster, for the rebuilding of the Reichstag didn't include a dome—it was the German Government who requested it. The result was an open cupola, reached by a series of elegant spiral stairways. It has been described as a structure which personifies the spirit of democracy.

RIGHT: The Oberbaumbrücke, built over the River Spree in the 1730s, links the districts of Friedrichshain and Kreuzberg. As these districts were once on different sides of the Berlin Wall, the bridge has come to symbolize the unity of the new Berlin.

LEFT: The Nikolaiviertel (Nicholas Quarter) on the banks of the River Spree is probably the oldest district of Berlin—the site of the medieval city. However, these buildings are all the result of a post-war restoration project by the East German government, and do little more than give a flavor of what the area once looked like.

DEM DEUTSCHEN VOLKE

LEFT: When the Reichstag was first completed in 1894, there was no inscription on the front of its façade. However, in 1916, the phrase "Dem Deutschen Volke (For the German People)" was added, against the wishes of the Kaiser. The inscription was retained when the building was rebuilt during the 1990s.

RIGHT: After the reunification of Germany in 1990, Potsdam and its palaces were deemed by UNESCO to be of world heritage status, and the palaces and parks were extensively restored. They are now a major tourist attraction.

LEFT: This iconic bust of the Egyptian Queen Nefertiti is the centerpiece of a collection of Ancient Egyptian artifacts which were first brought to Berlin in 1828, under the patronage and encouragement of King Friedrich Wilhelm III. When the Nefertiti bust was displayed in the collection in 1923, she was immediately dubbed "the beautiful Berliner".

RIGHT: The interior of the Berliner Dom (Berlin Cathedral). Although the late-nineteenth century cathedral was extensively damaged during the Second World War, the building was restored by the East German authorities from 1984–89, and the work was continued following reunification. The cathedral was reopened for Lutheran services in 1993.

LEFT: In 2005, the Holocaust Denkmal (Holocaust Memorial) was unveiled near the Brandenburger Tor (Brandenburg Gate)—a striking cemetery-like field of 2,700 concrete plinths. The monument was designed by American architect Peter Eisenmann as a fitting tribute to "The Murdered Jews of Europe".

RIGHT: The unification of Berlin into one city began as soon as German reunification was declared in October 1990. This was a major undertaking, involving the reorganization of Berlin's road and rail network, and her urban planning policies. In 2001, Mayor Wowereit speeded this process of unification by merging several of Berlin's districts, so they now spanned the old east-west divide.

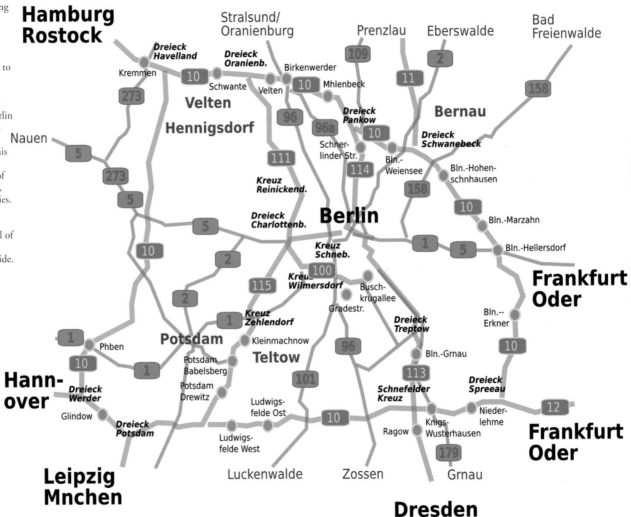

LEFT: The skyline of modern Berlin. During the Cold War, this area was a deserted wasteland, but after reunification it rapidly developed into a new metropolis, dominated by some of the most striking modern buildings in Europe. The most striking of these is the Sony Center, in the background of this view.

RIGHT: Since German reunification in October 1990, the Rotes Rathaus (Red Town Hall) has been the seat of Berlin's mayor, a post which has been held since 2001 by the Social Democrat Klaus "Wowi" Wowereit. The Town Hall is also the seat of Berlin's State Legislature, as the city is considered its own city-state within Germany.

BELOW: Following the reunification of Germany, West Berliners were able to enjoy the countryside surrounding their city, and the River Spree (shown here) and the River Havel have once again become popular weekend destinations. More adventurous Berliners travel to the Baltic coast near Rügen, or the beautiful area of forest and lakes known as the Spreewald to the southeast of the city.

RIGHT: The modern skyline of central and Eastern Berlin is dominated by the Fernsehturm (Television Tower), dwarfing the cupola of the restored Berliner Dom and the grand civic buildings of the eastern Unter den Linden and the Museumsinsel. After reunification this area once again became the civic heart of a unified city.

Picture Credits

Index

Dedicated to

Winnie and Dick

Fine Porcelain & Pottery

Fine Porcelain & Pottery

The best of the world's beautiful china

Stanley W. Fisher

Galahad Books

GALAHAD · BOOKS

Contents

Oriental wares

Japanese 'Eine' vase

This book is intended as a study of pottery and porcelain for those who claim no qualifications of a technical or historical nature but who approach the subject with a true appreciation of what is really beautiful. For this reason the illustrations have been chosen primarily because of their aesthetic appeal but also with the hope that the reader may perhaps be tempted towards a wider exploration of the subject and ultimately to the pleasures of collecting.

The cradle of pottery and porcelain making, so far as it affects the story told by this series of illustrations, was in the valley of the Yellow River of China, a region subject to prehistoric invasion by many alien peoples, and though much crude pottery was made as far back as the Chou period of 1120–249 BC, it was in the H'an period, beginning in the year 206 BC, that trade with foreign parts brought with it such techniques as lead-glazing from the Roman Empire and glass-making from Syria and Egypt, which served as spurs to the Chinese potters, both as regards technique and aesthetic beauty in form and decoration.

Then, during the Dark Ages of the third to the sixth centuries AD, repeated savage invasion and the need for basic survival brought the development of most art forms to a standstill. At the same time, with the ascendancy of Buddhism and the shaping of Buddhist art, notably in the forms of masterpieces in bronze and in sculpture, the craft of making beautiful ceramics slowly but surely developed until during the T'ang dynasty (AD 618–907) fine porcelain was made for Imperial use.

It was the custom during this period in Chinese history to furnish the tombs of important people with stoneware figures of men, women, horses and camels which would be expected to serve and entertain them in the afterlife. In fact, it was a custom which became so popular that it is recorded that in 741 the number of figures permitted in any one tomb was restricted by an Imperial order. Nevertheless, great numbers of horses and camels in particular have been excavated, both glazed and unglazed, some of them retaining their original colouring. The man standing on a bull, illustrated *left*, is humorously out of proportion,

Chinese T'ang figure AD 618–907

Chinese dish K'ang Hsi period

but typifies the grace and strong appreciation of movement which is characteristic of T'ang figure modelling.

Painting in cobalt-blue under the glaze was a technique learned from the potters of the Near East, and in China it reached perfection during the Ming dynasty (1368–1643) when fine white porcelain was the vogue, and was largely produced at Ching-tê-Chên, the ceramic metropolis of China. The bowl illustrated on *page 9* has restrained yet boldly flowing underglaze-blue decoration, and dates from the 15th century. At first this kind of fine porcelain was reserved for use in the Imperial palaces, but was later destined not only to be made for general use and for export to Europe, but also to be repeatedly copied during the centuries following, a factor which causes many problems of identification to modern connoisseurs.

The reign of the Emperor K'ang Hsi (1662–1722) has often been compared with that of his great contemporary, Louis XIV of France. The porcelain of the period was original in style, of fine design and magnificent decoration. *Left* is a ewer in the form of a horrific monster, in which we can see the cruel strength of modelling, so typically Chinese, allied to the beauty of coloured glazes and enamels. The creature is closely related to the kylin or Chinese unicorn, the Buddhist emblem of Perfect Goodness, which is one of two very similar beasts often seen either sculptured or painted on Chinese wares of all periods. The other is the Chinese lion or 'Dog of Fo', chosen it is said by the Buddha (proving his power over the King of Beasts) to guard his temples and to accompany him like a pet dog. The Buddha could change the lion into a little dog and back into a fierce lion when defence was needed against the forces of evil, a legend which manifested itself again in the 19th century when the Staffordshire potters made their large earthenware dogs, intended to stand guard on either side of a cottage hearth.

This typical 'Dog of Fo' illustrated *left* is decorated in a style to which the name of *famille verte* was given by the French, and which was developed during the K'ang Hsi period. The three main colours used were a soft yet brilliant green, a dark manganese purple of varying shades, and buff yellow; they were used either in the forms of glazes or of enamels, some-

Chinese ewer K'ang Hsi period 1662–1722

Chinese 'Dog of Fo' famille verte K'ang Hsi period

Chinese figure of a cat K'ang Hsi period

times with the addition of blue which was at first underglaze and later enamelled, and iron red. For their sensuous beauty the *famille verte* colours may well be compared with those seen upon English figures of the Ralph Wood variety.

In complete contrast, but of the same period, the beautifully designed, softly coloured dish on *page 9* is a fine example of Chinese reticence in decoration. It was not intended for export and so has no flat rim, and it is important to draw the distinction between the ornamentation of such a piece as this, which would be a prized possession of its

wealthy owner and the more crowded, often meaningless design of the decoration upon wares expressly intended for the use of ignorant foreigners. In the centre is the kind of garden scene much copied by European porcelain makers, with its flowering shrub, pavilion and fence. The four round border panels contain conventional lotus blossoms—a Buddhist symbol signifying purity.

Many animals and birds were included in the designs upon Chinese porcelain and were often Taoist or Buddhist symbols, or used in some sort of punning association. It is strange that cats are rarely seen. Even when

they were modelled they were usually of grotesque or humorous design. Since so much of the decoration on Chinese wares was based upon legend or myth, the neglect of the cat may perhaps be traced to the story that at Buddha's funeral, while all the other animals stood round weeping the cat turned its back to chase a rat. This is a most splendid K'ang Hsi example, typically posed and decorated in glowing but quite unnatural colours. It is cross-eyed like a Siamese, and the legend is that their squint was due to the original cat's gaze being fixed for ever upon the Golden Goblet of the Buddha.

Chinese pair of cats Ch'ien Lung period 1736–95

Many figures were decorated in the *famille verte* palette, often of great dignity and magnificence in the baroque style, though they do tend to be rather stilted in the modelling and lack the spontaneous vigour of the earlier models. Obviously the details of any figure, whether of pottery or of porcelain, must to some extent be obscured by the double layers of enamel and glaze, and the Chinese method of applying enamels directly upon the fired 'biscuit' was often used in order to overcome this difficulty. The sharply defined example *left* represents a warrior, and is of the K'ang Hsi period.

Wares painted with easily fusible enamels applied 'on the biscuit' are in fact among the loveliest of 17th-century Chinese porcelains. Large vases – this one is 29 inches in height – are exceedingly rare, and particularly attractive with the ideal combination of perfect shape and well-designed decoration. We see here a favourite style of design which cleverly combines delicate blossoms and gnarled tree-trunks with upthrusting, straight twigs. Although there is a superficial resemblance, this

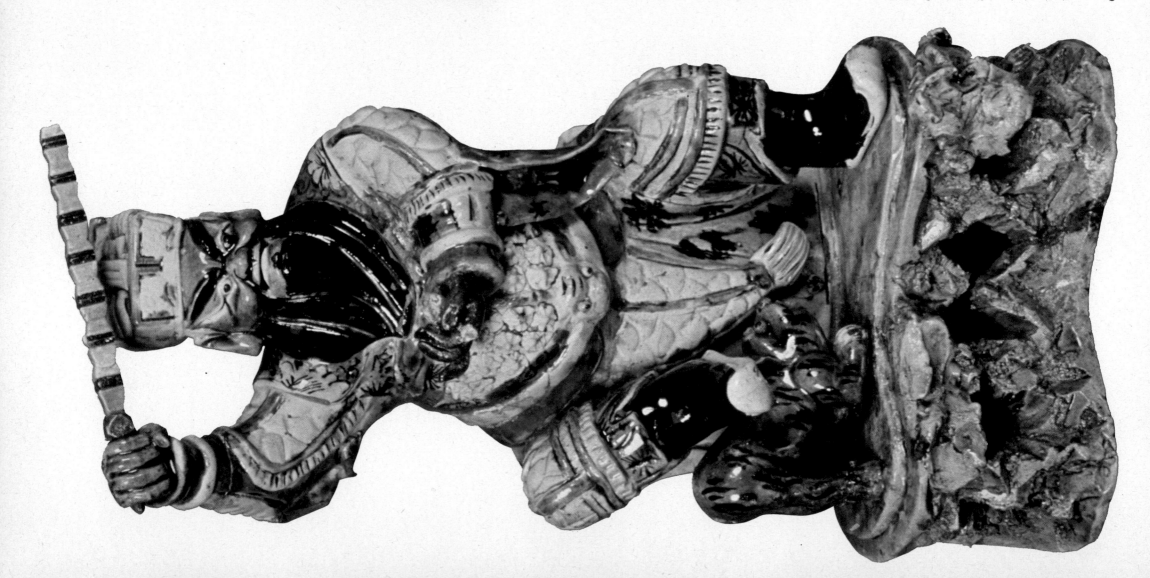

Chinese figure of a warrior K'ang Hsi period

kind of decoration is quite different from the *famille verte* overglaze enamelling. It is interesting to note that the vase bears the mark of the Emperor Ch'eng Hua (1465–87) though it was actually made during the reign of K'ang Hsi – a typical instance of the use of an earlier mark not with the intention to deceive, but simply to express reverence for age and beauty.

In strong contrast to the placid domestic cat on *page 11*, this unique pair, to judge from their colouring, are probably models of the savage Chinese desert cats which were discovered by Europeans less than 100 years ago. The vigorous modelling, the large size (16 inches in height), and the kylin-like, threatening expressions of this remarkable pair make them outstanding examples of the Ch'ien Lung period. This was a time, between 1736 and 1795, when although European demand for Chinese wares had reached its zenith and as a result many of them were designed to cater for a less educated taste, the Chinese potter still retained the inimitable, age-old skill in modelling which enabled him to produce masterpieces.

Chinese vase K'ang Hsi period, but with mark of Ch'eng Hua period 1465–87

Chinese blanc-de-Chine figure of Kuan-yin 18th century.

These include unsymmetrical arrangements of flower-sprays and branches of flowering shrubs, birds and animals, landscapes and domestic scenes, many of them enclosed within elaborate brocaded and diaper borders. The peony was frequently used to display the ruby-pink to best advantage, and all-over floral patterns were used in the manners of cloisonné enamels.

The most prized of all *famille rose* pieces are those which have been given the name of 'ruby back', because their undersides are covered with pink or crimson enamel. This lovely kind of porcelain is usually of eggshell thickness, extremely translucent, and enamelled in the clear-cut, calligraphic Chinese style which owes nothing to Western influence, although it was admired by European eyes. The painting on the plate illustrated *right*, is exquisite in its detail, is surrounded by intricately interwoven brocading, though not so elaborately as in the well-known 'seven-bordered' plates. This is a decorative style which was much imitated by the early porcelain makers at Worcester and Liverpool, and given the name of 'mandarin'. It usually featured Chinese ladies in garden or domestic scenes, anglicized and much elongated, and called by the unflattering name of 'Long Elizas' by English collectors.

During the 18th century armorial services became popular in England, and although the making and decorating of them was occasionally done (at Worcester in particular) the usual practice was for orders to be sent to China, accompanied by appropriate sketches of coats-of-arms. Much of the decoration was done at Canton on porcelain made at Ching-tê-Chên, in whatever style was in fashion in China at the time. Sometimes the china traders sent actual examples of the shapes to be copied, in silver at first but later in earthenware or even porcelain. Thus, in many English 'stately homes' we may see large sets of plates and oval or octagonal dishes, together with such un-Chinese articles as tankards, mustard-pots, ice-pails and so forth, made of a rather rough and grey-looking porcelain, and decorated in underglaze blue ('Blue Nankin'), *famille verte* or *famille rose*. The tureen

Something completely different – the placid, pure white figure of the Buddhist goddess Kuan-yin dates from the 18th century. It is an example of the kind of porcelain called *blanc de Chine* by the French, made at Tê-hua in the province of Fukien, which in fact was the only porcelain of significance made in China at that time other than at the great potting centre of Ching-tê-Chên. It was a porcelain, too, which was greatly admired in Europe, where it was imported in large quantities. Imitations of it were made at Meissen, and in 'soft paste' at Saint-Cloud, Chelsea and Bow, though no imitation has ever approached the rich and lustrous appearance of what is probably the most beautiful white porcelain ever made. Its colour varies between pure white and warm ivory, and is sometimes tinged with pink; the glaze is deep and soft. No photograph can convey these characteristics, but we can admire the serenity of the entire conception, the clear-cut, flowing lines of the pose, and the delicate, detailed modelling of the hands.

During the Yung Chêng period (1723–35) the *famille rose* palette largely replaced the *famille verte* on all but a few export wares. *See pages 2–3.* It took its name from an opaque, ruby-pink enamel derived from gold which had made its first appearance during the K'ang Hsi period. The supporting enamels were pale green, blue and a purplish-mauve colour called 'aubergine', with the occasional addition of opaque white.

Because so much export ware was of the *famille rose* type, the name of 'foreign colours' was given by the Chinese to the new colour scheme. Owing to the vast quantities of *famille rose* which came into Europe many characteristic styles of decoration are familiar to Western collectors.

Chinese famille rose plate 18th century

Japanese dish style of Kakiemon

and dish illustrated *below* are decorated with flower-sprays in the *famille rose* manner and were made during the Ch'ien Lung period of 1736–95.

Little is known about the fine porcelain which was first made during the 17th century in the neighbourhood around Arita, Japan. There is certainly a tradition that a Japanese potter named Shonzui visited Ching-tê-Chên in 1510, studied there, and took back with him to Japan a knowledge of making blue-painted porcelain and a supply of the necessary materials. Be that as it may,

European eyes have for a long time been misled by the 'Old Imari', decorated for export in dark blue, India red and gold, and by the 19th-century Japanese copies of Chinese wares which flooded the European market. One style of Japanese porcelain painting has nevertheless been familiar in the West for two hundred years, invented by a potter named Kakiemon, and freely copied at Meissen, Saint-Cloud, Bow, Worcester and Chelsea, usually in the well-known 'wheatsheaf', 'banded hedge' and 'quail' patterns. Illustrated *above* is a rarer, lovely example of this delicate style, painted

in soft shades of the typical Kakiemon colours of lilac blue, pale green and primrose yellow.

'Satsuma' may well be coupled with 'Old Imari' as being a name familiar to European collectors. It is commonly given to the once much-prized and nowadays again popular export wares of the Satsuma province, decorated with meticulously laboured patterns and extravagantly gilded brocades on a creamy, crackled base. Nevertheless, some of the rather earlier ware of this type, such as the 'Eiré' vase illustrated on *pages 6–7*, is well-designed and delicately enamelled and gilded.

Chinese armorial wares Ch'ien Lung period 1736–95

Continental tin glazed earthenwares

Dutch Delft plaque about 1680—1720

The practice of painting in colours upon a white 'tin-glazed' surface came to Europe from Mesopotamia and the southern shores of the Mediterranean into Spain, Italy and France in the 14th century. The glaze itself, applied to the surface of lightly-fired earthenware, was at first a secret which was carried from one country to another by wandering potters. Since the glaze did not become highly fluid in the kiln, as a lead-glaze does, decoration painted upon it did not run, though fused into it. The technique was revolutionized by the export of Chinese porcelain early in the 18th century, when, in order the better to imitate it, European potters developed a thinner kind of tin-glazed earthenware called *faience* in Germany and France, *maiolica* in Italy, and *delft* in Holland and England. The fine dish illustrated, made at Siena in Italy about 1510, has a typical border of interlacing branches – sometimes strapwork was used instead – and the clear-cut, beautifully drawn central subject of 'Abraham and Isaac' was probably painted by an artist named Benedetto. .

Nevers faience dish 'Bleu Persan' style period 1630–1710

During the 16th century wandering groups of Italian potters settled in southern Spain, in Antwerp, and finally in Nevers (or Nièvre) to establish tin-glazed earthenware factories in the Italian *maiolica* tradition. During the following century, however, the city's potters and decorators became famous as the originators of a distinctly French style, embodying the baroque taste of Louis XIV, and of translations of Chinese art forms which were independent of those used elsewhere. Among the many distinctive forms made in Nevers were pilgrim bottles such as those illustrated *left*, dating from *c* 1630–1710, painted in the style known as 'Persian decoration' with birds and flowers. A feature of Nevers painting in colours, always of great beauty, is the palette of bright green derived from copper oxide, a soft orange, a misty blue and a pale yellow, the perfect compatibility of which is well-exemplified in the photograph.

The Nevers decorators were pioneers among faience makers in their copying and adaptation of Chinese ceramic styles, and it has been suggested that they may have had Chinese originals before them as they worked. Much of the porcelain they imitated would of course be of the 'blue and white' variety and when the name 'Persian decoration' was coined by the first director of the Sèvres Museum, the type of painting seen in the illustration *right* was called *bleu persan*. The name may well be applicable both to 16th- and 17th-century Persian wares painted in opaque white on a blue ground, and to the similar work upon this dish, even though it has a distinctly Chinese flavour. The painter has, of course, assimilated the decorative use and value of the oriental birds and flowers and though his design is crowded, the brushwork is so delicate and the blue ground so luminous, that the result is satisfying and beautiful.

Faience was made in Rouen from about 1645, and became important when in 1647 a new factory under the direction of Edme Poterat was granted a 50-year monopoly for the whole of Normandy. Notable among the ware made during his management, which lasted until 1696, was 'blue and white'

Rouen faience dish 'Style rayonnant' decoration early 18th century

painted in the *style rayonnant*, so-called because of the symmetrical arrangement of the motifs radiating from a large central medallion, which after about 1710 often became a coat-of-arms. The dish *below* is an example of this kind of decoration, though the blue is here supplemented by red, a characteristic colour which was sometimes used also to vein leaves or for outlines instead of the more typical cross-hatching, as we see here. The design is admittedly mechanical, almost geometrical, and is based almost entirely on the octagon, yet at the same time it is so well-balanced, and in its

own way so restrained, as to be attractive.

The Strasbourg faience factory was founded in 1721 but as was the case at Rouen it was not until an outstanding director was appointed that distinctive, noteworthy wares were made. He was Paul-Antoine Hannong, who began his work in 1739. A feature of the faience made under his direction was a lovely range of new colours of the kind known as *grand feu* (because they could be fired at very high temperatures), which included a strong yellow, green and brick-red. Many gifted artists and modellers were engaged just before the middle of the century, and their work is to be seen in the forms of clock-cases, wall-fountains, and other rococo extravagances, with a wide variety of tureens modelled as vegetables, fruit or birds, such as the duck and pigeon models *below*, which may be dated *c* 1760. They are faithfully modelled, well-painted and quite endearing, and were possibly the inspiration for the many tureens and egg-boxes made by English earthenware and porcelain factories.

When the Lorraine factory at Niderviller was founded in 1754 the

Strasbourg faience tureens about 1760

best workmen and painters were brought from Strasbourg, as were many of the shapes and decorative styles. There was, however a definite leaning towards French styles rather than those borrowed from Germany. The tureen, cover and stand shown *right*, modelled in a restrained rococo style, are elegant and smoothly flowing, and the flower painting, most exquisitely done, is of the type known as *fleurs fines*. It was a style introduced at Meissen about 1740, copied from botanical engravings, and characterized by careful shading. The three pieces illustrated date from *c* 1755–70.

Probably the most interesting and

successful of all Niderviller wares are its faience figures, particularly those made in the 1750s and 1760s in the manner of a Strasbourg modeller named J W Lanz. These individually styled small figures of children, shepherds and other rustic types are finely moulded, even though the thick glaze tends to obscure the modelling. The toy-like quality of this kind of work is clearly to be seen in the illustration *over* of a country boy and girl of the period 1755–60. The soft flesh-tints, the subdued colouring of the striped chintz patterning of the costumes, and the flat pad bases painted to resemble grass are all characteristic.

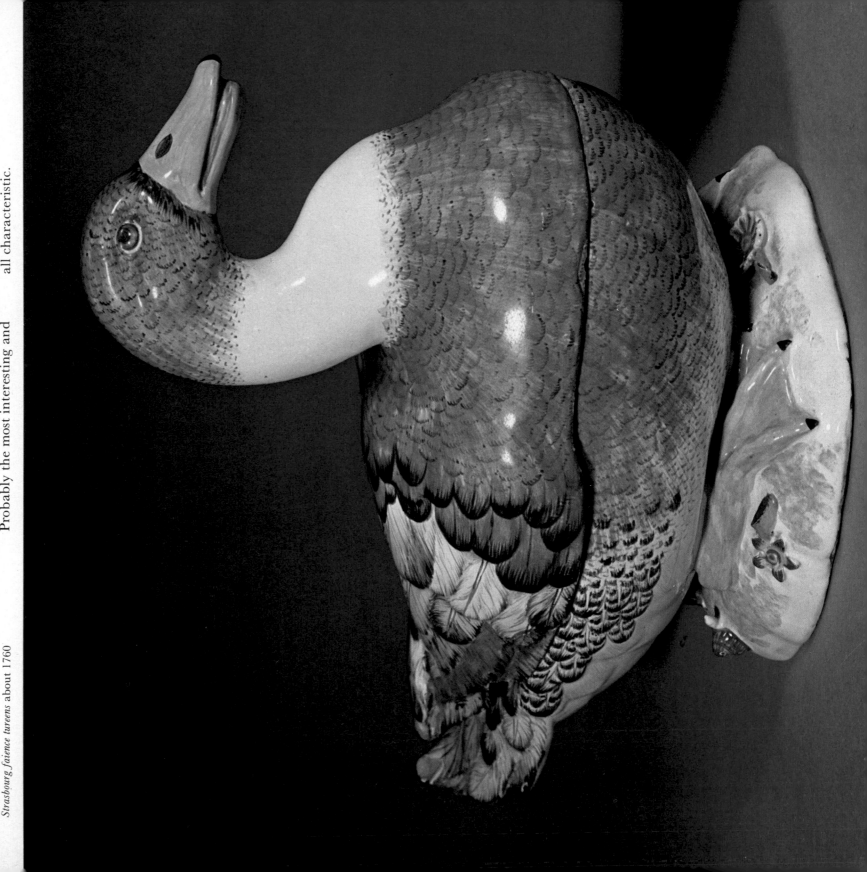

Strasbourg faience tureens about 1760

Niderviller faience tureen, cover and stand period 1755–70

The small town of Delft, near Rotterdam, was not among the first Dutch centres of faience making, but it rose to such prominence between about 1625 and 1650 in the making of tin-glazed imitations of Chinese porcelain that its name has been universally given not only to the Dutch wares but to those made also in England. The Delft potters were able to make them as light as the Chinese originals, while in addition they achieved a brilliance of colour often superior to that which was possible on 'hard-paste' porcelain. Above all,

Dutch Delft hyacinth vases 18th century

perhaps, the rapid growth of the industry was due to the new-found popularity of the Chinese 'Blue Nankin' which was brought into Europe in enormous quantities by the Dutch East India Company, founded in 1609. The Delft copies are probably the best made anywhere in Europe at that time, whether exact copies or patterned in the oriental manner, and they owe their beauty to the warmth of the white tin-glaze and the richness of the cobalt-blue. Among the Delft productions of the late 17th and early 18th centuries were shaped oval plaques such as that which is illustrated on *pages 16–17*. The drawing is exceptionally fine and detailed, but close examination of what is at first sight Chinese-style decoration reveals that the figures in the panels are more Dutch than Chinese.

On the whole, the Delft makers were clumsy modellers, and with such exception as shoes, cow-creamers, violins and bird-cages, which were Dutch in origin, their work in this regard was usually copied, not very successfully, from Chinese or Meissen models. The pieces illustrated represent a pair of pyramidal, tiered hyacinth-vases, perhaps the most noteworthy of all Dutch plastic work. They are original in the sense that they were not copied from the oriental, although they were clearly inspired by the shape of a Chinese pagoda. In its simpler form the lobed and handled hyacinth-vase, with its lid fitted with several tiers of cylindrical apertures and known as a 'finger vase', is a commoner Delft shape.

Early in the 18th century copies were made in Delft of oriental polychrome wares, notably of *famille verte* porcelain of the K'ang Hsi period and of Japanese 'Imari' ware. Then, as the century advanced, and pieces of *famille rose* became better known in Holland, new enamels were invented to reproduce the colour scheme to be imitated. Among the more important productions of the period were large 'garnitures' in Chinese style, which were made in sets of three covered vases and two beakers, an example of which is seen here, together with a pair of butter-tubs and covers whose shape is of course not Chinese at all, though all seven pieces are in the *famille rose* style.

Niderviller faience group period 1755–60

Dutch Delft garniture and butter-tubs 18th century

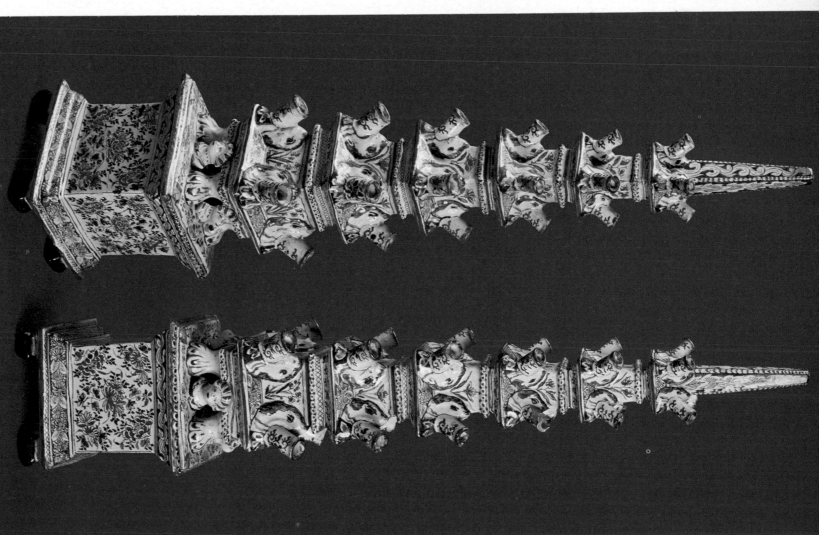

Continental porcelains

Meissen dish painted by Herold about 1730—35

Imitation porcelains known by the names of 'fritt' or 'soft paste' had already been made at Rouen and Saint-Cloud in France when the experiments of the physicist von Tschirnhausen and the chemist J F Böttger led to the foundation in 1710 of the Royal Saxon factory at Meissen, near Dresden. By 1720, under artist-director Johann Gregor Herold, production of true or 'hard paste' porcelain was in full swing. So began the creation of what was to be the accepted style in European porcelain decoration. Naturally enough, in common with every other kind of ware made in the West, much of it was at first painted in oriental styles, and the bottle and cover shown *left*, made about 1725–35, are a delicate and most beautifully reticent adaptation of the Japanese Kakiemon manner, the typical pale blue in particular being very fine. Indeed, the drawing is so accomplished that one is tempted to think that it may have been done by the Meissen master of this particular style, Adam Friedrich Löwenfinck.

When Augustus the Strong had the fancy to furnish his Japanese Palace with porcelain, the Meissen management engaged many skilled modellers to make figures, among them Johann Joachim Kaendler. He was a genius who understood in his vigorous modelling how to make the most of the play of light and shade in every hollow and on every projection. Some of his figures are of great size and he has been rightly acclaimed as one of the greatest of all ceramic modellers of animals and birds, which he fashioned from life. Many of his larger birds were left 'in the white', but others were faithfully enamelled, as we see *right* in this fine model of a woodpecker, nearly 11 inches high, and made about 1735.

At the time when Kaendler was making his incomparable figures, Herold was improving old styles and inventing new ones. His duty during his early years at the factory was perhaps above all to reproduce oriental wares to the king's satisfaction, or alternatively to invent variations of oriental themes. In later years he introduced what is one of the most lovely of all Meissen decorative subjects, the so-called harbour scenes with tiny figures and boats

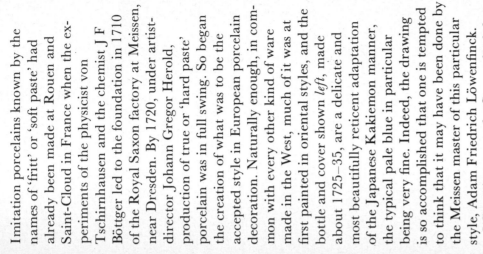

Meissen bowl and cover painted by Herold about 1730-35

by the seashore or in landscapes. This style is illustrated on *pages 24-5.* The dish is armorial and carries the lovely gilding which often accompanies Herold's work. It may be dated *c* 1730-35.

The beautiful handled bowl or *sucrier* and cover is another example of *chinoiserie* in Herold's style, delicately drawn but here not enclosed within tooled or lacework gilding, but reserved on a yellow ground, in a manner commonly used both for tablewares and for ornamental vases, some of them of large size. The king was extremely fond of coloured grounds, and his insistence upon them for display in his palace hastened their invention, for many had been perfected by 1725. So far as yellow is concerned it is possible that it had been mastered by 1727, since a vase so decorated, bearing Herold's signature, carries that date. Vases made for the king in this panelled style were marked with his initials AR in monogram form, a fact which has often been exploited by the makers of pseudo early Meissen reproductions.

About 1735 Kaendler began to model small figures which were in

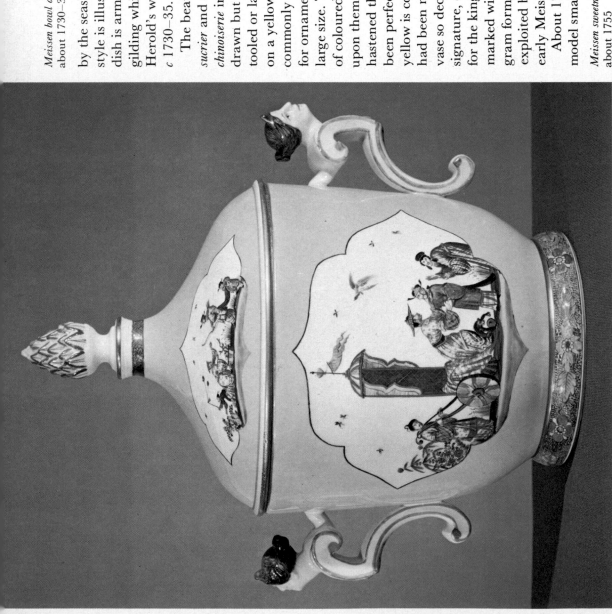

Meissen sweetmeat dishes modelled by Kaendler about 1755

Meissen Harlequin modelled by Kaendler
about 1740

complete contrast to the important
animals and birds demanded by the
king. Among these were figures of
characters in the 'Italian Comedy'
troupe of Angelo Constantine, which in
fact had earlier been the inspiration for
stoneware figures produced by Böttger.
Kaendler's first figure of this kind was
a 'Harlequin playing bagpipes', and

the 'Greeting Harlequin' *above*. Although
simpler in design, it well exemplifies the
strength of movement, rhythmic outline,
bright, almost hard colours and brilliant
glaze of the figures which for ten years or
so were the greater part of Meissen
output.

By the 1740s Meissen was producing
a bewildering variety of polychrome
domestic ware, several styles of which
are to be seen on *page 31*. The *chinoiseries*

continued in favour, in Herold's
manner, as did oriental flower and
Kakiemon subjects, while probably as a
result of a series of French engravings
sent to the factory in 1741, Watteau-
like subjects were introduced in the
style seen upon the coffee-pot, and
pastoral scenes such as that upon the
saucer. The deep crimson-purple
ground colour, like the yellow, was one
of the pigments favoured by the king.

Meissen 'Man with a Guitar' about 1745

Meissen tea and coffee wares about 1765

which were never discontinued, though in the 1770s attempts to compete with the growing rivalry of Sèvres was the cause of the development of stronger, harsher tones.

Among the smaller figures made under Kaendler's direction during the period c 1740–5 was a great variety of folk types — beggars, drummers, mapsellers, bagpipers, and so forth. They are characterized by simplicity of form coupled with boldness of modelling and their colouring is strong, yet sparingly used so as to allow the brilliant, highly-glazed white texture of the porcelain to show to best advantage. In the illustration of a 'Man with a guitar', 6¼ inches high, there is nothing but down-to-earth, robust vigour; the attention is not distracted by any fussy detail which is so alien to the true nature of porcelain.

By the year 1750, probably as a result of increasing competition from the rival factories at Vienna, Berlin, Höchst and Fürstenburg, figure-making at Meissen had become an industry, and though Kaendler modelled with his old brilliance, one detects a decline in the virility which featured so strongly in his earlier work. The illustration on *page 28* shows a pair of sweetmeat dishes — from a set of Seasons modelled by him *c* 1755. Their comparative restfulness is emphasized by the use of the pleasing tones of pale yellow and mauve which at that period had begun to be preferred to the striking, almost startlingly strong reds, yellows and black of earlier years.

Flowers have from the beginning been considered appropriate and popular as decoration upon porcelain, and have taken many forms. At Meissen towards 1740 the formal, conventionalized oriental varieties gave place to arrangements of naturalistic European flowers many of which have been traced to the illustrations in botanical works, which were known in Germany as 'teutsche Blumen' or 'Meissner Blumen'. They were at first stylized, but by about 1750 they had become warmer and more natural-looking, to be copied extensively by English decorators at Chelsea and elsewhere. The bouquets are reserved here upon the fine Meissen mazarine-blue ground, and it is interesting to note that the graceful

Meissen tablewares about 1740

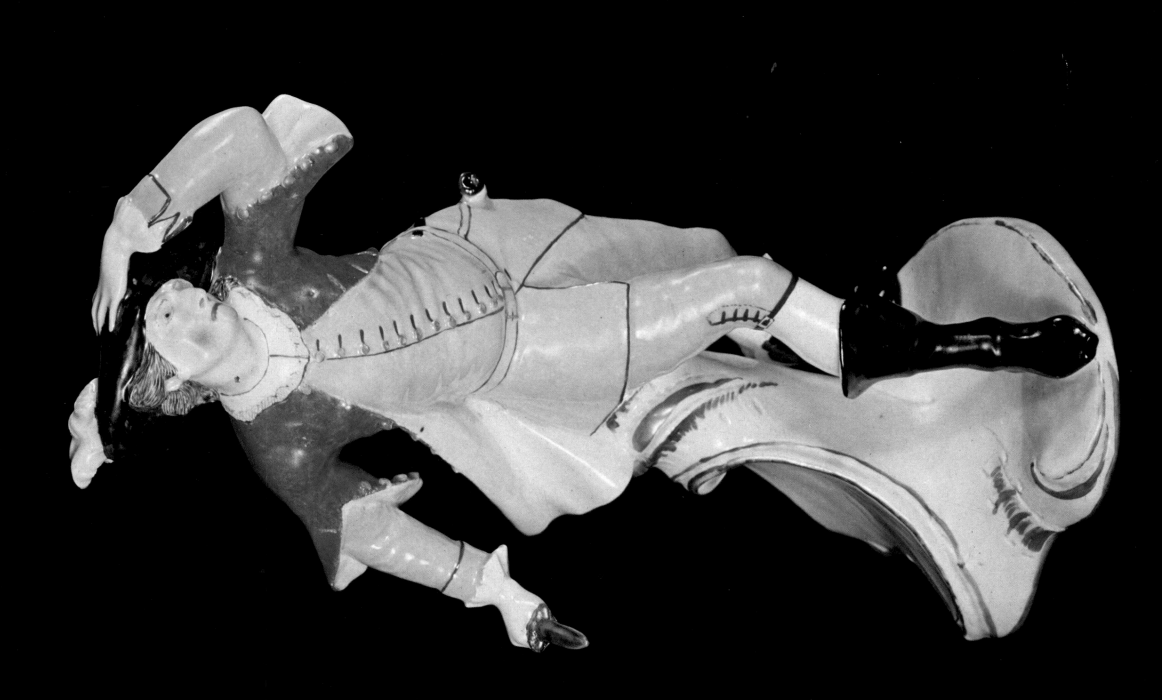

Nymphenburg 'Italian Comedy' figure about 1760

Vienna cup and saucer about 1730–35

In 18th-century Germany the secret of porcelain-making was jealously and strictly guarded, and the second oldest factory was started in 1719 in Vienna only with the help of a Meissen workman named Stölzel who had absconded to join Claud du Paquier, the proprietor of the new venture. Nowadays, such a great deal of forged porcelain is to be seen, much of it ostentatiously gaudy and extravagantly gilded, marked with the shield mark which was introduced in 1744, but in fact made long after the closure of the factory in 1864, that it is appropriate here to illustrate a cup and saucer of the true du Paquier ware, made *c* 1730–5. The decoration is simple, with hardly any gilding, but porcelain of this period is among the rarest and the most beautiful of early German ware. The tall cup, sometimes two-handled, is typical and the decoration in formalized, somewhat stiff oriental style, features a characteristic strong red.

A small factory was founded in Berlin in 1752 by Wilhelm Kaspar Wegely, who was encouraged by Frederick the Great. It closed down in 1757. In 1761, having purchased Wegely's formula for making 'hard-paste' porcelain, a Prussian financier named Gotzkowsky was able to use it only with the aid of artists, modellers and other workmen from Meissen. It would seem that Frederick had long desired to own a porcelain factory, and in 1763 he purchased the Berlin concern, which has remained State property until the present day. For the most part, styles and decoration were much influenced by Meissen and Sèvres, but the illustration *right* shows another style of Berlin decoration which features architectural subjects. Rather surprisingly this is a most meticulously drawn view of Apsley House, London.

In Bavaria porcelain making was begun in 1755, first at Neudeck and six years later at Nymphenburg, when the factory was moved to new premises

shapes of coffee-pot, tea-pot, cream-jug, teapoy and covered *sucrier* (sugar-basin) are those which were adopted in earthenware and in porcelain by English potters. The two pots were of course copied from silver shapes, and the service of which they were part was made about 1765.

Berlin plate about 1765

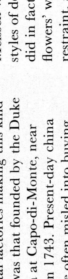

Capo-di-Monte beaker about 1745–50

Meissen was always in mind as regards styles of decoration, the French artists did in fact render their 'German flowers' with greater delicacy and restraint, and in course of time a degree of excellence was reached in every branch of ceramic art which effectively ousted the German factory from its long-standing pre-eminence. The tea-pot, *left*, dating from *c* 1750, is a beautiful example of the work of the Vincennes flower-painters.

We have already seen, in the early history of porcelain making in Europe, that chemists, modellers, and decorators moved from factory to factory, taking their secrets with them. The result, so far as modern collectors are concerned, is that positive identification based on paste and decoration often presents problems. Thus, because the 'soft paste' of Vincennes and early Sèvres was made to the formula of François Gravant, who with other workmen had moved from Chantilly, there is great similarity between the porcelains made at the several factories. The tastefully

Sèvres biscuit group about 1755–60

Vincennes tea-pot about 1750

in the palace grounds. Much tableware was made, but it was the work of the Swiss modeller Franz Anton Bustelli between 1755 and 1763 which brought fame to the factory, and which nowadays is held in high regard. The illustrated figure of the Italian Comedy character 'Capitano Spavento' on *page 32*, 7½ inches high, is a typical example of his distinctive work, which was always modelled in flowing, rhythmic curves and planes, usually rising uninterrupted from flat bases. Many figures were left 'in the white', as are some of the products of the modern factory, which are based on old models, and when colour was used it was applied in flat washes of strong colour.

At the time when Meissen and other European factories were able to make 'true' porcelain, using china-clay and china-stone in the oriental manner, many others were apparently unable to discover the secret, and instead used various mixtures of what was virtually powdered glass and white clay to make their artificial or 'fritt' porcelains which in England have for a long time been

known as 'soft paste'. Among the continental factories making this kind of ware was that founded by the Duke of Parma at Capo-di-Monte, near Naples, in 1743. Present-day china lovers are often misled into buying pieces bearing the mark of the N surmounted by a crown, usually found on highly-coloured figure subjects in high relief, or small figures, believing them to be genuine antique products of the factory. The truth is that in the mid-19th century the Capo-di-Monte moulds were acquired by the Doccia concern, whose output has been very considerable. The genuine porcelain made by the old factory is not only of extremely fine quality, but is very rare indeed. The graceful beaker shown *above* is decorated exquisitely in the oriental style and was made during the period *c* 1745–50.

'Soft-paste' porcelain was made successfully at Vincennes in France from about 1745 onwards, before a new factory at Sèvres was finished and put into use in 1756. The fame of the early ware rests upon the incomparable beauty of its *pâte tendre* paste, as it was called, and though the enamelling of

Sèvres bowl, cover and stand about 1760–70

Vincennes plate about 1745–50

Vincennes bowl, cover and stand about 1745

decorated plate illustrated *left* is a case in point, but it may nevertheless be ascribed to the Vincennes period of 1745–50 on the authority of the Musée de Sèvres. The central motif, a landscape with a castle, is painted in the typical light Vincennes style and was perhaps a loose but effective translation of the Meissen harbour and landscape scenes.

The painting of panels reserved on coloured grounds is the most characteristic and perhaps the most splendid of all Sèvres decoration, to be imitated in England at Chelsea, Worcester and, later, at Coalport in particular, as and when it was possible to make the colours. This example of Vincennes porcelain made *c* 1745 *right* has the earliest of these beautiful grounds, the underglaze *gros bleu*, dark and attractively uneven, which was invented as early as 1749. The gilding which edges the reserves of birds is of the exquisitely drawn type which was later copied, with the blue ground, on 'gold anchor' Chelsea porcelain. So far as Sèvres ground colours are concerned, the *gros bleu* was followed by the *bleu celeste*

(turquoise) in 1752 and the *jaune jonquille* (yellow) in 1753, while the famous and much-imitated *rose Pompadour* (pink) was introduced soon afterwards.

Most of the early figures made at Vincennes and Sèvres were coloured, but a few were left white, and glazed. In 1751, however, art director Jean-Jacques Bachelier invented a new (unglazed) 'biscuit' porcelain which

thereafter with few exceptions was used for figure making. Very many models were made, all of them original, for the lovely white paste was eminently suited to the purpose. As the illustration on *page 35* shows, detailed modelling is not obscured by glaze, neither is well-balanced, finely-tooled form spoiled by the distraction of shining highlights.

Above is another example of the

characteristic Sèvres production of perfected ground colour, gilding and painting in reserves. The 'German flowers' are not so delicately rendered or so carefully drawn as they would have been in earlier years at Vincennes, but the gilding is superb. It is not in this instance lightly pencilled as is sometimes the case, but is thickly applied, delicately chased, in some places burnished, and in others left soft and dull. This is exactly the style of decoration which was to be imitated successfully during the early 19th-century 'Sèvres revival' period at Coalport.

The making of 'hard-paste' porcelain began at Sèvres in 1769, though both kinds of paste were used concurrently until 1800. The use of the new material increased production, but much beauty was lost because at the same time new

Sèvres garniture of vases about 1780

and often rather pretentious styles were introduced. The magnificent garniture of vases illustrated, though dating from *c* 1780, is 'soft paste', the central one being 20 inches high. The decoration, in the 'oil painting' manner of the period, is one example of the mythological designs which had by this time largely replaced the lovely pastoral scenes of earlier years. The elaborate gilding is entirely in keeping with the painting, and features a restrained use of the so-called 'jewelling', a process using drops of enamel, which is said to have been invented by Cotteau about 1780. It was probably done here by the gilder Étienne-Henri Le Guay, who worked at Sèvres during the period 1749–96.

During the last years of Louis XV fine Sèvres porcelain was given as diplomatic presents, many to foreign royalty. Among these was a fine

garniture of vases, one of which is illustrated *right*. It was made and decorated to the order of Gustavus III of Sweden in 1780, to be presented to the Empress Catherine II of Russia. It is 19½ inches in height and enamelled in the then popular style, in which panels of decoration in the oil-painting manner were reserved on coloured grounds. In this case the ground was laid in *bleu de roi*, the paler, more even enamel which replaced the underglaze *gros bleu* at some time before 1760, and the lovely foliate gilding was done either by Le Guay or by Le Grand. Happily here the porcelain is not entirely covered by the decoration, which had in fact become at this time more important than the material carrying it.

Sèvres vase 1780

Chinese bowl 15th century Ming dynasty

This book is intended as a study of pottery and porcelain for those who claim no qualifications of a technical or historical nature but who approach the subject with a true appreciation of what is really beautiful. For this reason the illustrations have been chosen primarily because of their aesthetic appeal but also with the hope that the reader may perhaps be tempted towards a wider exploration of the subject and ultimately to the pleasures of collecting.

The cradle of pottery and porcelain making, so far as it affects the story told by this series of illustrations, was in the valley of the Yellow River of China, a region subject to prehistoric invasion by many alien peoples, and though much crude pottery was made as far back as the Chou period of 1120–249 BC, it was in the H'an period, beginning in the year 206 BC, that trade with foreign parts brought with it such techniques as lead-glazing from the Roman Empire and glass-making from Syria and Egypt, which served as spurs to the Chinese potters, both as regards technique and aesthetic beauty in form and decoration.

Then, during the Dark Ages of the third to the sixth centuries AD, repeated savage invasion and the need for basic survival brought the development of most art forms to a standstill. At the same time, with the ascendancy of Buddhism and the shaping of Buddhist art, notably in the forms of master-pieces in bronze and in sculpture, the craft of making beautiful ceramics slowly but surely developed until during the T'ang dynasty (AD 618–907) fine porcelain was made for Imperial use.

It was the custom during this period in Chinese history to furnish the tombs of important people with stoneware figures of men, women, horses and camels which would be expected to serve and entertain them in the after-life. In fact, it was a custom which became so popular that it is recorded that in 741 the number of figures permitted in any one tomb was restricted by an Imperial order. Never-theless, great numbers of horses and camels in particular have been excavat-ed, both glazed and unglazed, some of them retaining their original colouring. The man standing on a bull, illustrated *left*, is humorously out of proportion,

Chinese dish K'ang Hsi period

Chinese T'ang figure AD 618–907

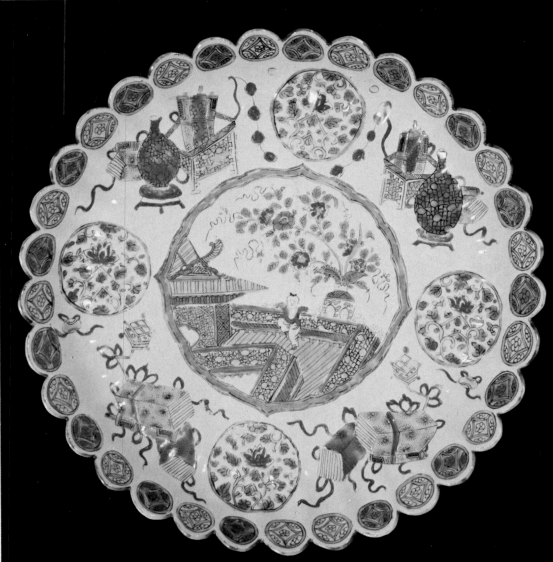

9

The practice of painting in colours upon a white 'tin-glazed' surface came to Europe from Mesopotamia and the southern shores of the Mediterranean into Spain, Italy and France in the 14th century. The glaze itself, applied to the surface of lightly-fired earthenware, was at first a secret which was carried from one country to another by wandering potters. Since the glaze did not become highly fluid in the kiln, as a lead-glaze does, decoration painted upon it did not run, though fused into it. The technique was revolutionized by the export of Chinese porcelain early in the 18th century, when, in order the better to imitate it, European potters developed a thinner kind of tin-glazed earthenware called *faience* in Germany and France, *maiolica* in Italy, and *delft* in Holland and England. The fine dish illustrated, made at Siena in Italy about 1510, has a typical border of interlacing branches – sometimes strapwork was used instead – and the clear-cut, beautifully drawn central subject of 'Abraham and Isaac' was probably painted by an artist named Benedetto.

Nevers faience bottles 'Persian decoration' 1630–1710

Meissen bottle and cover Kakiemon style
about 1725–35

Imitation porcelains known by the
names of 'fritt' or 'soft paste' had
already been made at Rouen and
Saint-Cloud in France when the experiments of the physicist von
Tschirnhausen and the chemist J F
Böttger led to the foundation in 1710
of the Royal Saxon factory at Meissen,
near Dresden. By 1720, under artist-
director Johann Gregor Herold,
production of true or 'hard paste'
porcelain was in full swing. So began
the creation of what was to be the
accepted style in European porcelain
decoration. Naturally enough, in common with every other kind of ware
made in the West, much of it was at
first painted in oriental styles, and the
bottle and cover shown *left*, made
about 1725–35, are a delicate and
most beautifully reticent adaptation
of the Japanese Kakiemon manner,
the typical pale blue in particular
being very fine. Indeed, the drawing
is so accomplished that one is tempted
to think that it may have been done by
the Meissen master of this particular
style, Adam Friedrich Löwenfinck.

When Augustus the Strong had the
fancy to furnish his Japanese Palace
with porcelain, the Meissen management engaged many skilled modellers
to make figures, among them Johann
Joachim Kaendler. He was a genius
who understood in his vigorous modelling how to make the most of the play
of light and shade in every hollow and
on every projection. Some of his figures
are of great size and he has been rightly
acclaimed as one of the greatest of all
ceramic modellers of animals and
birds, which he fashioned from life.
Many of his larger birds were left 'in
the white', but others were faithfully
enamelled, as we see *right* in this fine
model of a woodpecker, nearly 11
inches high, and made about 1735.

At the time when Kaendler was
making his incomparable figures,
Herold was improving old styles and
inventing new ones. His duty during his
early years at the factory was perhaps
above all to reproduce oriental wares to
the king's satisfaction, or alternatively
to invent variations of oriental themes.
In later years he introduced what is
one of the most lovely of all Meissen
decorative subjects, the so-called harbour scenes with tiny figures and boats

Meissen woodpecker modelled by Kaendler
about 1735

English earthenwares

Coverham Abbey, in Coverdale, Yorkshire.

Wedgwood Queen's Ware about 1773–4

Buff-ware mask jug London 14th century

Slip-ware 'Toft' dish about 1680

In medieval England pottery was made wherever suitable clay was to be found, and it varied in the firing from area to area, and in colour from red to buff, yellow or even black. Some of it was covered by a lead-based glaze, which could be stained by mixing in copper filings to give greens ranging from yellowish moss-green to dark cucumber. The potter was uninfluenced by any foreign methods or styles, yet his products, intended solely for utilitarian use, have a dignity and aesthetic value which many connoisseurs claim to be lacking in the more sophisticated porcelains of later centuries. He had no mechanical aid other than some crude form of the potter's wheel, and he was at the same time potter and decorator, using perhaps a nail to scratch or 'incise' a pattern, 'impressing' a motif into the unfired clay with a seashell, 'applying' little pads of shaped clay in a contrasting colour, or even adding washes of liquid clay or 'slip'. Some of these techniques are to be seen in the fine 'mask jug' illustrated, which dates from the 14th century, and which was found in Bishopsgate, London. Jugs of this kind were the ancestors of the well-known 'Toby' jugs of late 18th-century Staffordshire.

So far as is certainly known, the first notable earthenware to be made in England's great centre of the ceramic industry, the 'Potteries' in Staffordshire, was what we call 'slip-ware', produced towards the end of the 17th century. The body of the ware was made of clay which fired to buff or red, and decoration was added by applying 'slip' stained to a contrasting colour, in washes, lines or dots, just as one might ice a cake. Alternatively, two colours of 'slip' might be 'marbled' together with a wire brush. Finally, the iron content of the lead-glaze resulted in a yellowish tinge to the whole. The best known and perhaps the most decorative of these wares are the large, round dishes which bear names, the commonest of which is Thomas Toft; though others are known, it is not yet certain whether they were those of the maker or of the recipient. The stately example illustrated was made *c* 1680.

Though Staffordshire had great advantages as a potting centre by reason of the presence of abundant clays of

Wrotham 'tyg' dated 1651

43

many kinds, plentiful supplies of coal for firing, and easy access by road or, later, by a good canal system, there were other 17th-century potteries making very similar ware to the 'Toft ware' described above. Among them, according to fairly reliable contemporary records, was one at Wrotham in Kent. Illustrated on *page 43* is a tyg, a particular kind of four-handled mug, which was apparently a distinctive Wrotham form. It is dated 1651, and other dated examples of this purely English form, crudely and heavily potted yet undeniably handsome, have also the actual place-name.

The more sophisticated earthenware called delft, the contemporary relation of continental tin-glazed faience and maiolica, was made in London by potters from Antwerp as early as about 1571, but by about 1630 English forms of the ware had been developed, at first painted in the styles of 'blue and white' Chinese porcelain, which of course it was intended to rival. The well-proportioned vessel *left* is a posset-pot, made probably at Fulham *c* 1670–1710, from which syllabubs, caudles and sack-possets, which were very popular at that time, were consumed. The elaborate cover is typical, the bird on the knob sometimes being replaced by a crown, and the blue-painting is a very fair imitation of the Chinese style. It is interesting to note that silver posset-pots of the same period seldom have spouts, and it has been suggested that this may reflect the drinking customs of different classes of society.

Though much early London delft was painted in the oriental style, other pieces bear subjects which include flowers and fruit, designs of spirals and whorls, ships, English kings and biblical events. Among these are large chargers which were made for decorative use, to stand upon buffets or to hang upon walls. Some are called 'blue dash chargers' because their edges bear broad radiating strokes of blue, red or green, though in fact one sometimes finds alternative edgings of linear patterns, of the kind to be seen in the illustration. The subject of this fine charger is 'Mary Magdalen', set against a background possibly of London buildings, since the piece is of London origin. Apart from the impor-

London delft mug 1642

45

English delft bottle and plates period c 1649–1790

tant fact that it is dated 1687, it is unusual because it has an embossed rim, the yellow-painted bosses of which were pushed up from beneath in the manner of Dutch delft.

The earliest forms of London delft bearing English inscriptions, some of them Christian names and surnames, date from *c* 1628 onwards. These include posset-pots such as that previously illustrated, wine bottles and straightsided or barrel-shaped mugs such as the example on the *previous page* which was made in 1642, probably at Southwark. The blue handle and bands are found on many mugs of the period, but the decoration, though extremely effective, is an unusually free translation of oriental motifs. The practice of making mugs, plates, jugs and other pieces for presentation to individuals on the occasions of births or marriages was an early one, and the proud possessor of this handsome mug was Ann Chapman.

The accurate identification of English delft made mainly at the potting centres of London, Bristol and Liverpool is often very difficult, and

the three pieces illustrated *above* are presented rather as types than as typical of any particular factory, though all were probably made at Lambeth. The bottle is dated 1659 and is of the kind intended for table use, usually marked in blue with the word 'Sack' (dry sherry) or more rarely 'Whit' (white wine) or 'Claret'. The plate may be dated *c* 1720–40, and is one of a set of six known by the name of 'Merry Man', the inscription thereon being a line of a doggerel verse which is continued over the complete set. The polychrome plate is an example of the latest Lambeth delft. The probable recipient has had her name given to the pattern, though in fact it is to be found on pieces made fifty years earlier.

The two handsome plates in the next illustration are both examples of painting in the oriental manner. The left-hand one, which may be dated *c* 1720, is an object lesson in what is known as the 'delft-painter's style'. The name of this particularly bold kind of brushwork owes its origin to the fact that it was necessary because of the powdery surface of the unfired tin-glaze, and it is interesting to see its

retention by artists who later painted upon porcelain. The blue-painted example is attributed to Bristol, and it is dated 1747 on the back. Its border is decorated with white slip in what is known as the *bianco sopra bianco* technique – though the ground here is not white but effectively slightly blued – and the Chinese scene is particularly restrained.

Both these next plates bear decoration in the distinctive palette of brilliant blue, yellow, green and red which has the name of the 'Fazackerly Colours' because it is said that a mug so painted, initialled T F and dated 1757 was presented to a Thomas Fazackerly by a Liverpool delft-maker. The plate on the left may be dated *c* 1750, and its design is a typically amusing anglicization of a Chinese scene. The same may be said of its companion, made *c* 1760, and here again it is interesting to note that each decorator had his own particular method of translating the Chinese trees, flowers, water, figures and, of course, the ubiquitous zigzag fence.

English delft plates about 1720–47

Liverpool delft about 1750–60

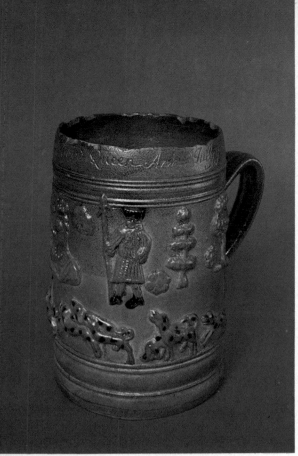

Salt-glazed stoneware tankard dated 1729

In 1693 a potter of Fulham named John Dwight was granted a patent by Charles II to make 'salt-glaze' stoneware. In brief, his ware was glazed by the volatilization of salt introduced into the firing kiln at a high temperature, resulting in an almost matt surface, only slightly glistening, and having the appearance of an orange skin. The tankard *above*, which may well have been made by Dwight himself, clearly shows the characteristic brown colour, the thick and heavy structure and the crudely moulded applied decoration. Nevertheless, there is considerable, insidious beauty in its very crudity and

Salt-glazed stoneware tea-pots mid-18th century

massive strength. In addition, and in common with a number of similar tankards in various collections, it can be exactly dated by the incised legend which encircles it below the rim. This reads – 'Drink to the pious Memory of Good Queen Ann, July ye 25: 1729'.

A pure white form of salt-glazed stoneware was produced as early as *c* 1720, strong, clean-looking, and admirably suited to the making of domestic wares. Dwight even made the earliest known figures of it, strongly modelled and accurately detailed, and by the use of finely-cut moulds, exquisite and delicately fashioned dishes, plates and other utilitarian pieces were produced. Then, by about 1740, because white salt-glaze had attained an excellence comparable with true porcelain and was so thin as to be almost transparent, decoration in colour was in full swing, carried out in enamels which stand out jewel-like upon the stoneware body. Illustrated *right* is a very lovely cream jug, modelled in a silver shape with a 'sparrow-beak' lip, and painted with well-spaced bouquets and sprays of conventionalized English flowers in just the same manner as much contemporary porcelain made at Worcester and Lowestoft. The inscription on this dainty little jug, which was made somewhere in the Potteries, reads – '*D.S.A.M.*, one Jugg more and then [17]66'.

Many beautiful tea-pots were made in coloured salt-glaze, two of which are shown *below*. One is buff in colour, and is decorated by means of a process known in the Potteries as 'sprigging', in which separate reliefs were made by pressing pads of clay into moulds,

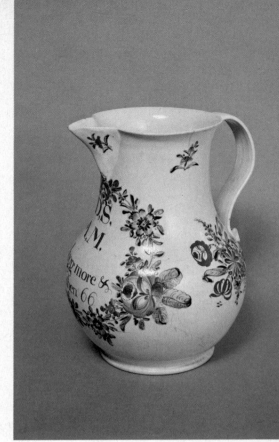

Salt-glazed stoneware cream-jug dated 1766

afterwards attaching them to the ware with 'slip'. The process clearly permitted the use of an endless variety of colour. Many beautiful coloured grounds were used on salt-glaze, including brilliant but uneven blue, pink, turquoise and green, together with a large variety of diapered and brocaded ones. Upon these grounds, either in reserves or not, all kinds of painting were applied, including flowers, landscapes, Chinese and European figure subjects and portraits. The tea-pot seen here bears a portrait of Frederick the Great reserved upon a ground patterned with royal ermine.

It is impossible to identify the work of the salt-glaze painters, since no

marks or signatures were used, but a number of surviving pieces bear brushwork which helps us to distinguish certain hands. The finest work, perhaps, was done by two Dutchmen who according to contemporary records set up their enamelling kilns at Cobridge in the Potteries. The tea-pot illustrated *right* may very well have been decorated by them: certainly the pastoral subject is in their style, and the colours are typically vivid and jewel-like. The painting is in the *famille rose* manner, and a notable feature is the use of the 'crabstock' handle and spout which are typical of so many tea-pots of this kind, which may be dated *c* 1765–70.

What may be considered to be the ultimate development of artistic salt-glazed stoneware began in 1815, when John Doulton founded his factory at Lambeth, thus laying the foundation of a business which is famous throughout the world. Then, in 1850, Sir Henry Doulton engaged a skilled band of artists, notably to carry out the distinctive style of incised decoration shown on the largest vase illustrated *right*. It is 17 inches high and it was made in 1895. The horse subject was the work of Miss Hannah B Barlow and F C Roberts. The central vase is an example of *pâte-sur-pâte* technique (painting with coloured 'slip') in this case carried out by Eliza Simmance in 1877, and the third is an early 20th-century piece decorated in the same manner by F C Pope.

Hannah Barlow, her brother Arthur, and her sister Florence were the first of the Lambeth artists to be engaged, and were the pioneers of a considerable number of equally skilled decorators who followed them. Nevertheless, the beautiful etchings of animals done by Hannah, whose work is seen here again, not on decorative vases but on equally well-designed utilitarian wares, are quite unique in ceramic art. It was fortunately the practice at Doultons for artists' monogrammed initials to be incised beneath pieces for which they have been responsible, together with dates. Thus, we know that all three pieces illustrated were made in 1882, and that Lucy Barlow did subsidiary work upon the coffee-pot and bowl.

Doulton stoneware dated 1882

Contemporary with the making of white salt-glazed stoneware, the Staffordshire potters, led by Thomas Whieldon of Fenton, developed a lovely lead-glazed earthenware, using a similar mixture of white clay and ground flints, which came to be known as 'cream-ware'. It was admirably suited to the making of simply decorated domestic wares, but like salt-glaze its smooth surface was a perfect vehicle for more splendid painting, when desired, both on utilitarian and ornamental wares, using a palette of new enamels designed to suit it. The tea-pot illustrated *below*, made *c* 1760, has an obvious kinship with a salt-glaze form. Its decoration is restrained yet entirely satisfying, featuring a design of Chinese 'fish-roe' diaper and conventionalized flowers carried out in brick-red.

Whieldon began potting at Little Fenton about 1740, and took Josiah Wedgwood into partnership in 1754. From then until 1759, when the latter left to found his own business in Burslem, the two potters were responsible for many innovations, and it is not always easy to decide which of the two introduced such wares as 'tortoiseshell' cream-ware with the glaze stained and mottled with grey, green, black, blue and yellow, and 'pineapple' ware in the shapes of cauliflowers, melons and, of course pineapples, in lovely green and yellow glazes. Nevertheless, the name of Whieldon is commonly associated with that of John Astbury as a pioneer maker of a large range of rather crude figures, while he himself led the way in developing 'sprigging' and the making of 'agate' or 'marbled' ware. *Above left* is a marbled tea-pot of Whieldon type, made *c* 1755–58. Its somewhat bizarre beauty was obtained by colouring clays which were then sliced and blended together to imitate natural stones.

The particularly beautiful jug illustrated *right* is an apt and typical example of the 'cauliflower' cream-ware previously mentioned, introduced at the time when Wedgwood and Whieldon were working together, with the result that attribution may be credited to either according to the opinions of different authorities. Whatever the case,

Cream-ware tea-pot about 1760

'Cauliflower' cream-ware jug about 1754–60

50

the contrasting of the cream colour and
the green to such beautiful effect was a
stroke of genius, particularly when
allied to such accomplished, clear-cut
modelling as may be seen here. The
green is a translucent glaze, derived
from copper, which was extensively
used on medieval wares, and which
for some reason fell into disuse until
revived by the two potters in question.

Wedgwood's triumph alongside
other makers of salt-glaze, delft and
other kinds of serviceable everyday
ware was his introduction of a harder,
thinly-potted cream-ware *c* 1765–7.
This he did under Queen Charlotte's
patronage, and accordingly he gave it
the name of 'Queen's Ware'. Josiah
paid particular attention to the beauty
and suitability to purpose of his forms,
which he decorated with pierced and
moulded patterning, printing and
enamelling. The illustration shows
three pieces with over-glaze printing of
the kind which was at first applied outside the factory, much of it in Liverpool.
The stately coffee-pot, shows a rural
scene. It was made *c* 1775 and the oval
dish with its feather-moulded edge a few
years later. It is interesting to see that
the tea-pot, which is decorated with the
'Death of Wolfe', is similar in shape to
those made of salt-glazed stoneware
and ordinary cream-ware.

Though 'Queen's Ware' was used for
quite ordinary, everyday services and
other tablewares, its intrinsic beauty
was such that in 1773–4 a large service
of nearly a thousand pieces was made
for the Empress Catherine II of Russia.
This was decorated in purplish black
at Chelsea under the direction of
Thomas Bentley, Wedgwood's partner,
the subjects being English landscapes
and country houses. The crest of a frog
was painted in green in the border,
hence the name of the 'Frog Service'.
The illustration shows what was
evidently a 'trial' plate painted in polychrome, and another from the actual
service. On each is one of the many
simple borders of husk-pattern, berries,
laurel leaves and other foliate designs
which often formed the only decoration
on typical cream-ware.

Wedgwood was without doubt the most outstanding figure in the story of English ceramics, and among the many kinds of ware which he invented, and which were copied throughout the Potteries, the lovely, technically perfect 'jasper ware', introduced *c* 1774–5, is best known. This fine white stoneware, stained at first in blue and sea-green, and decorated with applied and carefully tooled and undercut reliefs, was later made in both light and dark blue, lavender, sage-green, olive-green, lilac, yellow and black, and rarer pieces may incorporate several of these colours. In 1777 another kind of 'jasper' was introduced, called 'jasper dip', in which only the surface of the ware was coloured; two pieces are illustrated on *page 52*. The applied decoration, in the classical style Wedgwood so loved, was designed by eminent artists, among them James Tassie and John Flaxman.

In his admiration for the classical style, Wedgwood realized that a local Staffordshire black stoneware, called 'black Egyptian ware', was ideal not only for tablewares but would also be well-suited to the making of vases in the Greek 'Etruscan' style. Accordingly, about 1767 he introduced his perfected version of it, calling it 'black basaltes' and describing it as 'a fine black porcelaine'. The vase illustrated was No. 1 in the factory 'shape book' of 1770, and apart from the beauty of form which is so apparent, one can see very clearly the outstanding merit of the material itself, which was capable of taking on a most attractive dull gloss when burnished. Vases of this kind were the first productions for which the new body was used. Some were decorated with lightly fired metallic gold, while others were painted with designs in red, or red and white.

The 'black basaltes' body was ideally suited to the making of figures, since apart from its surface sheen it was exceedingly hard and could be sharply modelled and tooled. This striking figure of 'Mercury on the Rock', made in 1786, is a beautiful example of this kind of ceramic sculpture, standing 18 inches high. Others include a series of busts of classical and contemporary authors, and a well-known 'Voltaire' in the Victoria and Albert Museum in London. Some years ago the author had occasion to examine a very large and fine 'bronze' figure of Bacchus which had been in the owner's family for many years. To everyone's amazement, it was not bronze at all, but a specimen of 'black basaltes' made faithfully to imitate the metal by the admixture of metallic powder in the body.

It is interesting to see how Josiah Wedgwood and his successors at Etruria, always improving and perfecting, and in so many instances the leaders of ceramic style and taste, were themselves sometimes obliged to follow the dictates of popular demand. Their contribution to the demand for 'Japan' patterns which was so marked early in the 19th century is illustrated in the part tea-service shown on *page 53*, made to compete with the products of Worcester, Spode and Derby. The 'chrysanthemum' pattern, applied on a 'Queen's Ware' body, is nevertheless comparatively restrained and does not over-burden the white paste or detract from the beautiful line of the pieces.

In their copying and imitation of continental figures our early English

Wedgwood black basaltes vase about 1770

Wedgwood black basaltes figure 'Mercury on the Rock' 1786

54

porcelain makers catered for the higher strata of society, whereas the Staffordshire potters for the most part made what were virtually image toys, in a purely native style, to be sold for pence at a cottage door. Many were cheaply produced in large numbers by child labour, and indeed many are childishly crude both in conception and in execution. Countless backstreet factories in particular employed no skilled modellers or decorators, though certain classes of figures such as those made by the Wood family and by Pratt are much more refined and sophisticated. The anonymous Staffordshire red squirrel illustrated, made of cream-ware *c* 1790, shows the bold generalization demanded by the material, and the artlessness wherein lies the attraction of many 'Staffordshire figures'.

During the late 18th and early 19th centuries the Industrial Revolution brought in its train a demand by rural folk in particular for increasing amenities. They still could not afford to possess, or had no close acquaintance

Staffordshire egg-boxes about 1780–1800

with fine porcelain, but they were 'in the market' for finer earthenware substitutes for it. The handsome pair of egg-boxes on *page 55* was made somewhere in Staffordshire *c* 1780–1800, very much in the style of faience originals, and is most carefully and accurately modelled and decorated, and doubtless once graced the table of some yeoman farmer.

Among the finest Staffordshire figures which were in effect the poor man's porcelain were those of the so-called 'Walton School', a typical example of which is illustrated. John Walton is said to have begun making figures *c* 1790, gay and attractive models, cheerfully coloured, and usually of somewhat sentimental character. His intention, so far as his material and the skill of his modellers allowed, was to imitate those made at Chelsea and Derby, even to the sometimes quite elaborate and typical bocages such as we see here. His subjects, like this group of a rustic family which may be dated *c* 1820–30 were naturally of the kind which would appeal to countryfolk, for whom they were made in considerable quantities, not only by Walton but by many of his contemporaries.

In Victorian times 'chimney ornaments' were made in endless variety, including what are known as 'Staffordshire cottages' such as those illustrated. These took the form of castles, churches, cathedrals and of course cottages. Some were pastille-burners with removable roofs and open chimneys, some were money-boxes, and some were simply ornamental. It must be remembered too that much earthenware ceramic art of that period was commemorative, catering for a public which demanded ware or figures featuring popular heroes or personalities, notorious events, and so forth, the more sensational the better. Thus the castles, the cottage and the villa seen here, as usual bedecked with flowers and quite charming, might well represent the scene of some bloody siege, or the home of a notorious murderer. *See page 58.*

Staffordshire cottages mid-19th century

In just the same way as the chimney
ornament was the poor man's equi-
valent of the porcelain figure, so was
'lustre' his substitute for gold and silver.
And here again, the lustring process
perfected *c* 1790–1800, using platinum
chloride to give a metallic silver sheen,
and gold to give copper, pink or gold,
was a purely English invention. The
lustre effect derived from gold varied
between copper or golden yellow on
brown earthenware, while on a white
or cream body it was pink, varying
between pale tints and ruby depending
upon the thickness of the coating.
Illustrated here are representative
pieces of fine pink lustre, including
two wall-plaques of typical Sunderland
type, a Swansea 'cow-creamer', and
a beautiful small jug decorated with
white reliefs. The larger jug is a specimen of Leeds 'pink resist' lustre, so-called
because the patterning was shielded by
an adhesive solution which resisted the
metallic bath, but which could be
washed off, with the unwanted lustre
upon it, when the object was dry. Lustre
could be applied all over, in splashes, in
bands, or with reserves left clear to
contain decoration in printed or painted
form, or combinations of both.

The rare beauty of the finest 'silver
resist' lustre is seen to fine advantage in
this illustration. The well-proportioned
'bough-pots' were made in Leeds,
most intricately and delightfully
patterned, and the two jugs, one of
them moulded with masks of 'Tragedy'
and 'Comedy', and the other painted
with a robin, need no description to
emphasize their quality. In all four
pieces the ground is white, but even
finer and of course rarer specimens are
those with coloured grounds of blue,
brown or yellow. The small mugs are
examples of the simpler kind of copper
lustre, bearing the sketchiest of
painting. Lustred figures were produced at many centres, some of them
treated 'all over', and others partly
lustred and partly enamelled, such as
this colourful example made by
Dixon's of Sunderland, one of a set of
four Seasons. All the pieces illustrated
date from the period *c* 1790–1810.

Various lustre ware about 1790–1810

Even more than the 'cottages', the subjects of the Victorian mid-19th-century 'chimney ornament' figures form a quite comprehensive commentary on the social life of the time. The only public entertainment, at least in rural areas, was the circus, and many circus subjects were produced, including representations of lion, tiger and leopard trainers, performing elephants, horse training and riding, performing dogs and dancing bears. The illustration *below* is of the elaborate group which probably represents the 'Lion Queen' Ellen Bright, who was killed during a performance in January 1850, here accompanied by her two assistants. It is what is known as a 'flat-

back', a type generally popular from about 1840 onwards, so made as to simplify manufacture and cut costs; this was perfectly acceptable since only the front needed to be modelled and decorated, the white, flat back being against the wall.

So many popular heroes, politicians, sportsmen, and criminals were immortalized in the form of 'flat-backs' that it apparently became customary to use the same model to represent different characters, thus making for cheaper production. Only the decoration is different, so that identical figures are known whose identity as Wellington or Napoleon, Washington or Benjamin Franklin, and General or

Staffordshire chimney ornament Lord Raglan about 1855

Staffordshire chimney ornament 'Lion Queen' about 1855

Staffordshire chimney ornament The Rescue *by Sampson Smith about 1855*

a wealth of other vivid enamels, and hardly any gold. Later, one might think strangely, much less colour was used apart from flesh-tints, black and gold.

One of the few known makers of Victorian chimney ornaments was Sampson Smith, working from 1858 onwards. He did not generally use any mark, but much of his work may be identified because many of his moulds still exist, and the example illustrated, titled 'The Rescue' and made *c* 1855, suggests that his modelling was well above average, particularly that of the quite expressive faces of the characters. The pattern of the girl's dress is most carefully and delicately painted, and in fact the often elaborate patterning of costume, flags and so forth is a feature of the better 'flat-backs'. It should be mentioned here, if only as a hint to collectors, that after Smith's death in 1878 the business was carried on by his various successors until 1918, and that figure making, using original moulds, was revived again in 1948, though with new styles of colouring and with a distinctive mark.

Admiral Napier is indicated only by their names being painted or gilded on the bases. The 'Lord Raglan' shown *left* is also named, though so far as is known the model was not used to represent any other character.

The example *right*, as usual quite crudely modelled, and cheaply produced in a three-piece mould, represents a 'Tiger Hunter' made *c* 1845–50. Blood sports were extremely popular in Victorian England, and figures featuring them were especially so if representing any exotic variety, the bloodier the better. One can imagine the care with which some anonymous decorator drew in the gash on the horse's hindquarters. The decoration of the 'flat-back' followed a marked fashion, at first featuring a strong blue,

Staffordshire chimney ornament Tiger Hunter *about 1848*

English, Welsh and American porcelains

Swansea mug about 1816

Chelsea farmyard clock 'red anchor' period about 1755

Chelsea Fisherman and Drunken fisherman 'red anchor' period about 1755

CHELSEA

Chelsea porcelain was made from about 1742 to delight fashionable London society with elegant, beautifully painted wares which were designed to compete with the finest that could be produced on the continent. The greatest period of the factory, during which the mark of a tiny red anchor was used, was between *c* 1750 and *c* 1760, and Chelsea figures of the 'red anchor' years are among the loveliest ever made. Meissen models were the inspiration for many of them, although once again the English versions are often superior by reason of the soft colours and the sparing use of gilding upon the beautiful, soft white paste.

The two lovely plates illustrated here were made during the period 1750–60. Many of the early designs were of German or Japanese invention, and exemplified here are the restrained and

Chelsea plates 'red anchor' period about 1750–60

delicately coloured Kakiemon styles, freely adapted, and probably not copied directly from the Japanese, but from Meissen versions. The moulding of the larger piece is extremely beautiful (and totally ignored by the painter) and the brushwork upon each most meticulously and delicately applied. Moreover, though this cannot be judged from a photograph, the total effect of the fine enamelling upon the Chelsea 'soft paste' is more pleasing than the appearance of the 'hard-paste' Meissen equivalents.

Nothing could be daintier or more admirably demonstrate the beauty of fine porcelain than the octagonal Chelsea tea-bowl and saucer of the 'red anchor' period *right*. The names of the early factory artists are unknown, but the charming landscapes here are in the style if not by the hand of the 'Fable painter', so-called because many of his creations were based upon Francis Barlow's edition of *Aesop's Fables*. His distinctive brushwork is to be found on porcelains other than Chelsea, but in this illustration we see the typical use of scattered Meissen flowers and insects which often accompany the river scenes and landscapes which, again in imitation of the

Chelsea scent-bottle 'gold anchor' period about 1760

Chelsea clock 'gold anchor' period about 1758–69

German works, were painted sometimes in crimson monochrome, the
'purple landskips' of the sale catalogues.

The particular kind of 'red anchor'
porcelain illustrated *above left*, made
about 1755, is known in several forms.
There is a pigeon-house, referred to in
the sale catalogue of that year as a
'magnificent perfume-pot in the form
of a Pidgeon House with pidgeons, a
fox etc.', a clock-case with a dog and
chickens, and another clock-case in the
form of a pigeon-house, complete with
dog and fox. There is that kind of
humour here which is more usually
associated with earthenware than with
fine porcelain, yet at the same time
there is all the vigour of the 'red
anchor' years, and the slight colouring
which so enhances, even in a photograph, the beauty of the white paste.

The features which make Chelsea
'red anchor' figures so outstanding are
seen to perfection in these two models
of a 'Fisherman' and a 'Drunken

Chelsea tea-bowl and saucer 'red anchor' period
about 1750–60

63

Chelsea 'botanical' plate 'red anchor' period about 1755

fisherman', both of which are after Meissen originals. They are examples of how the Chelsea modellers translated the turbulent, often harsh character of the German models into a more restful mood which was to some extent indigenous in their soft paste material, and which was enhanced by the delightfully soft colouring. It is generally accepted that a Tournay modeller named Joseph Willems, who worked in Chelsea during the period *c* 1755–66 set the style for Chelsea figure modelling, and it is interesting to note that what appears to be a well-known companion figure to the 'Fisherman', the 'Fisherman's wife', is recognized as his work.

The painting of botanically accurate flowers was a common and popular style of decoration upon much later English porcelains, notably at Derby and Swansea, but the freedom and beauty alike in drawing and in colour of Chelsea 'red anchor' examples, such as that illustrated *left*, far surpasses any later work. Contemporary sale catalogues refer to 'Sir Hans Sloane's plants'. Sloane was a physician to Queen Anne, and an expert botanist, cultivating in his 'Chelsea Physic Garden' 50 plants a year on behalf of the Royal Society. Many of the flowers upon these attractive 'botanical' plates were copied from hand-coloured illustrations in 'Figures of Plants', published by Philip Miller, the Apothecaries' Chelsea gardener, in 1756. Many are more scientific than decorative but some, such as the example illustrated here, were cleverly adapted to the circular shape of the article, often with the added attraction of exquisitely drawn, judiciously placed butterflies, moths and insects.

The tureens illustrated bear the tiny red anchor of the same fine middle period of the Chelsea factory. This kind of vessel, in this case in the forms of a melon, a lettuce, a cos lettuce and a cabbage, was inspired by Meissen. Others known include rabbits, plaice, swans, asparagus, cauliflowers, and a hen (described in a 1755 factory sale catalogue as a 'most beautiful tureen in the shape of a hen and chickens big as life'). These colourful pieces are now rare collectors' treasures, safely housed behind glass, but they were intended

Chelsea tureens 'red anchor' period about 1750–60

Chelsea Madonna and Child 'red anchor' period about 1755

for everyday table use, and were in fact copied in earthenware in the Potteries.

The qualities of the work of the 'red anchor' period and in particular the delicate yet bold Chelsea modelling are seen to perfection in the beautiful 'Madonna and Child' shown *above*, referred to in the 1755 factory sale catalogue as 'an exceeding fine figure of a Madonna and a child with a cross in its hand'. Apart from its beauty, the group is probably a unique representation of this subject in early English porcelain.

A change took place at Chelsea in about 1758 when the paste was modified by the addition of calcined bone-ash. The result was that it was possible to make more elaborate and sometimes larger figures, while at the same time decoration became much more elaborate and splendid, with a more prolific use of rich gilding. So began the period *c* 1758–69, which is known as the 'gold anchor' period, because the anchor factory mark was painted in gold by the gilders when they had finished their work. The illustration of a clock of this period is worthy of close study, because it illustrates so many characteristic 'gold anchor' features. See *page 63*. It stands upon the type of scrolled base, often resting upon feet, which became very popular; there is a wealth of projecting detail, made possible by the tougher paste; the colours are brighter, and there is gilding. The beautifully decorated face of the movement is the final touch of the decorator's skill.

The tiny scent-bottles, needle-cases, seals, *bonbonnières* etc. modelled in animal or human form, known as 'Chelsea Toys' are among the most highly valued 'gold anchor' pieces, despite their small size, which varies between about $2\frac{1}{4}$ inches and $4\frac{1}{2}$ inches in height. A typical example is illustrated on *page 63*, dating from *c* 1760. It features a child, but others are modelled in the forms of birds, animals, Chinese figures, friars, cupids, flowers, fruit, Italian Comedy characters, and mythical subjects. Flower-sprays in tooled gold are common under the bases of scent-bottles, and many 'toys' have French inscriptions, which probably accounts for the fact that they have often been mistaken for Sèvres productions. Another common feature of scent-bottles is the gilt mount and chain to the stopper, which here is in the form of a dog, while others include flowers, birds or flambeaux.

DERBY

Porcelain was made in Derby as early as *c* 1750, and though little is certainly known about the very earliest wares, an auction sale held by the 'Derby Porcelain Manufactory' in December 1756 included 'A Curious Collection of fine figures.... after the finest Dresden models'. Illustrated is a fine group of 'Lovers and a Clown', which may be dated *c* 1755 and which was copied from a Meissen model by Kaendler. Other Derby versions of the same group have bocage, but all belong to the 'patch mark' type of figure made *c* 1755–70, so-called because of the presence on the flat base of three or four dirty-looking, unglazed patches left by the pads of clay used to support the ware in the glazing kiln.

Figures of birds were made at several early English porcelain factories, including the Chelsea copies of Meissen, the fanciful ones of Bow, Plymouth hard-paste models, and dainty, colourful Derby creations such as the pair of blue tits pictured *above*, only 2¾ inches in height and made *c* 1760–5. Birds are among the rarest of Derby figures, less brightly coloured perhaps than those made at Chelsea, and less accurately modelled than, for instance, the amazingly lifelike Doughty birds of modern Worcester. They rely rather

Derby 'Lovers and a Clown' about 1755

upon a certain naïve, toy-like simplicity for their attractiveness. The stable bases are left white except for the sparse bocage, in order to let the porcelain speak for itself.

The vase shown *over* was made at Derby about 1820 during what is known as the Bloor period. It was a time when competition from Spode and the Worcester factories was causing financial difficulties, one effect of which was the making of the kind of 'Japans', crowded and showy, which smack of the fairground and did little to enhance the Derby reputation. At the same time much fine work was done, as we see here. The shape is a typical one and the flower painting, though inclined to be mannered rather than naturalistic, as the fashion was at that time, retains some of the Billingsley tradition, and was done by Thomas Steele, painter of fruit and flowers. The typical arabesque design upon the base is of a type often used to decorate tea and other domestic wares.

The beautiful little figure of a boy *over* was made about 1765, at a time when a new, creamy-white body and colourless glaze had been perfected. The pedestal base raised upon scrolled feet picked out in gold and dull turquoise had by now replaced in favour the pad base of earlier years – though still bearing 'patch marks' – and the bocage, showing the typical tubular Derby flowers, is more pleasingly restrained

Derby vase about 1820

than on later figures, upon which it was often carried to such extremes that the significance of the modelling was lost. It is instructive to compare the rather wooden pose with the vigour and movement of the Meissen work previously described and illustrated.

This lovely two-handled bowl and stand is an example of the early Derby tableware made during the period

Derby bowl and stand about 1755–60

1755–60. The decoration is restrained, the flower painting rendered in a purely English style which was not copied from Meissen, but which has a kinship to Chelsea. To the collector the handles are distinctive – they have been likened to 'inverted wish-bones' – and the chocolate-brown edges are purely decorative, although the Chinese ones from which they were copied were intended to prevent chipping. It should perhaps be stressed that the name of

Derby figure of a boy about 1765

'Crown Derby' is properly given to wares made since 1890, though in fact a crown was incorporated in factory marks from about 1775.

In the old Derby pattern book of figures and groups No. 227, according to John Haslem (*The Old Derby China Factory, Workmen and their Productions*) was a 'Pair of Grotesque Punches'. The original inspiration for

Derby 'Grotesque Punches' about 1770–75

New Hall plate about 1815

NEW HALL

In about 1781 the patent rights of
Richard Champion of Bristol to make
hard-paste porcelain were purchased
by a Staffordshire syndicate which in
1782 set up the New Hall factory at
Shelton. From the beginning shapes
and patterns were simple in the
extreme and output was by and large
confined to useful wares, mainly tea-
services. Every collector is familiar
with the range of distinctive, moulded
New Hall shapes, though in fact both
they and the patterns used upon them
were sometimes shared by other
contemporary Staffordshire factories.
Occasionally, however, one finds a
fairly early specimen more carefully
decorated than was normal, and the
illustrated tea-pot, *c* 1800, is notable for

its gilding and for its well-painted view
of Dover Castle.

About 1812 the New Hall company
changed over from making hard-paste
porcelain to introduce a type of bone
china, much softer and more mellow,
and very like that made by Chamber-
lains at Worcester and indeed by many
other concerns in the Potteries. At the
same time, although the emphasis was
still upon making useful wares, using
shapes popular at the time, much more
ambitious and carefully painted
decoration was successfully attempted.
The plate illustrated, made about 1815,
is a typical example; the blue ground is
of good quality, the gilding well-
designed and applied, and the colours
used in the pleasingly sentimental
group in the centre were carefully
chosen to blend with those used by a
fruit-painter whose work is often seen

upon the later New Hall wares.

The *sucrier* (sugar-bowl) and cover
here are good enough in style and
quality to pass as Worcester of the same
period, were it not for the fact that they
bear the printed mark of 'New Hall'
within a double circle of the years
c 1812–20. The decoration is one of the
New Hall versions of the sort of 'Japan'
patterns which were so popular at that
time and, like the two examples
illustrated previously, the pieces are of
an excellence, particularly in the
technical accomplishment of the design
and the brushwork, which so often
surprises collectors whose judgment
of the ware is based upon the earlier,
often so sketchily decorated hard-paste
productions.

New Hall tea-pot about 1800

New Hall sucrier and cover period 1812–20

SWANSEA

At a time when other porcelain makers were using a standard 'bone china' paste, the perfectionist William Billingsley set up a small factory in 1813 at Nantgarw in Wales to make his own incomparably lovely ware. He spent a year there, moved to Swansea, and then back to Nantgarw about 1817, and finally gave up what had from the start been a hopeless venture. His beautifully translucent, mellow porcelain was difficult to fire, and kiln losses defeated him. The illustration is of a delightful cabinet cup, never of course intended for use. It was decorated by Thomas Pardoe, a painter of flowers in what has been described as a 'wet' style, who worked as a freelance decorator and who also painted Swansea, Worcester and Coalport porcelains.

William Billingsley was an extremely skilled china-painter as well as a technician, and whether at Nantgarw, Swansea or Coalport (where he finally moved in 1820) he was much occupied in teaching to the staff his own peculiar style of flower-painting. His method of wiping out highlights to expose the porcelain beneath has all too often been taken as proof of his work, although specimens actually decorated by him are extremely rare and for the most part well-documented – the Swansea plate shown *left* is such a piece.

Though much painting upon Swansea porcelain was done by skilled specialists, there had to be a wide range of stylized, easily and cheaply produced patterns which could be decorated by comparatively unskilled workers, and which were used mainly on tea or dessert services. One of these, called the 'Mandarin' pattern, illustrated on *pages 60–1*, was clearly adapted from the Chinese, though its designer could not resist placing a European building, complete with its high wall, in the background. The outlines of the pattern are printed, the enamels being washed in somewhat unskilfully by hand. This obviously useful, quick aid to the decoration of ware was used by practically every contemporary factory and should not necessarily be condemned as inferior. Always provided, of course, that the printed design is good in itself.

Rockingham tray period 1830–40

ROCKINGHAM

An earthenware factory was founded
c 1745 at Swinton in Yorkshire, but
after many changes in ownership porcelain was not made until *c* 1826, when
the concern was given the financial
support of Earl Fitzwilliam. The ware
was of the soft-paste variety, beautifully
soft and mellow, but always liable to
ruinous failure in the firing kilns. This
fact, together with the expensively
extravagant style of much of the
decoration, led to the factory's closure
in 1842. Among the lovely wares made
during a comparatively short life, many
figures both in unglazed white biscuit
and in enamelled forms were produced,
of which the 'Captain Cook' shown
here is a rare example, featuring the
vivid blue which is to be seen on many
specimens, and the equally characteristic gold line around the plinth.

In addition to the innumerable
array of tea, coffee, dinner and dessert
services made at Rockingham, and
the many types of spill-vases, handled
baskets and figures, a number of
large trays or plaques of the type
illustrated, 16 inches by 14 inches in
size, was produced. This particularly
lovely specimen, marked with the red
griffin, is notable for the excellence of
the painting upon it, which was done
by Thomas Steel and signed by him.
The Rockingham proprietors engaged
the best possible decorators, many of
them from other factories, and Steel's
work is also to be seen upon porcelains
made at Derby, Coalport and by
Minton's at Stoke. Thomas, whose
skill was inherited by his sons Edwin
and Horatio, undoubtedly had no rival
as a painter of fruit and flowers, and
he painted insects equally well. It
should be noted that the correct spell-
ing of his name, which is often mis-
spelt with a final 'e', is shown in his
signature here.

Rockingham 'Captain Cook' about 1830–35

Benington (USA) figure of a lion about 1852–58

AMERICAN WARES

It is interesting to observe that the story of 'red-ware', the first kind of colonial pottery which was made in the United States in the late 1600s, in many ways parallels that of English 17th- and early 18th-century earthenwares. For example, local clay was used by nomadic potters, the bodies and lead-glazes were coloured for decorative effect, considerable use was made of 'slip' in the manner of English 'Toft' ware, and the art of 'sgraffito' (designs scratched through a slip coating to show the body beneath) was well-known. In turn, too, styles changed

Royal Worcester vase and cover 20th century

as colonists came from England and the continent, while in addition, as in England, regional characteristics in religion or ways of life had considerable influence on the types and on the decoration of the wares produced. Apart from such early ware, colonial Americans imported all their finer ceramics from the Far East, England, France and Germany, and no real attempt was made before *c* 1825 to establish a ceramics industry. Illustrated here is a remarkably fine figure of a lion, nearly 11 inches long, which has evident kinship to English models made by the 18th-century Wood family, though it was made much later, between 1852 and 1858, by Daniel Greatbach, working at Bening-

ton, Vermont.

About 1820 the signs were that the ready availability of foreign porcelains, particularly English and French, was falling off. The porcelain trade between the Old and the New Worlds was steadily decreasing, and although after the Revolution abortive attempts were made to make porcelain, credit for the first successful venture is given to William Ellis Tucker, who in Philadelphia founded a factory which began work in 1825, and where French types of ware were produced until *c* 1838. Thereafter more and more porcelain manufactories were established, until by 1875 the United States had its own flourishing industry. This ambitious and most successful 'Electra'

Union Porcelain Works (USA) cup and saucer
about 1875–6

pedestal was made at about this time, designed by Karl Mueller and made by the Union Porcelain Works at Greenpoint, New York. It is no less than $42\frac{1}{2}$ inches in height, and its design was clearly influenced by Wedgwood's classical style. Certainly, Josiah himself would have commended its well-balanced design, and the sharp crispness of the applied relief ornamentation.

Union Porcelain Works (USA) 'Electra' pedestal
about 1875

So far as shapes and decoration are concerned, American porcelains made during the period *c* 1825–75 might as often as not have been produced at any contemporary English factory. It may be, in fact, that the necessary spur to original thought was provided by the Centennial Exhibition at Philadelphia in 1876, after which original styles, particularly in artistic wares, revolutionized the industry. At the same time, many of the old techniques were re-introduced, including the Chinese *sang-*

de-boeuf (or 'ox-blood') glazes, the crackled effects of the Japanese, and the use of metallic lustres and patterned 'slip' decoration. The 'Liberty' cup and saucer *above* was one of the choice pieces displayed at the Centennial, made by the Union Porcelain Works. Both technically and aesthetically it leaves nothing to be desired, and particularly effective, as a foil to the splendid modelling and gilding, is the use of the soft *pâte-sur-pâte* technique in the style of the English Minton factory.

Bibliography

Gray, Basil   Early Chinese Pottery and Porcelain 1953
Honey, W B   The Ceramic Art of China and other countries of the Far East 1945
Jenyns, Soame   Later Chinese Porcelain 1951

Honey, W B   European Ceramic Art in 2 vols: Historic Survey (1949) and Dictionary (1952)
          French Porcelain 1950
Landais, H   French Porcelain 1961
Wynter, H   An Introduction to European Porcelain 1971

Fisher, S W   English Ceramics 1966
Godden, G A   Victorian Porcelain 1961
          An illustrated encyclopaedia of British Pottery and Porcelain 1966
Hagger, R G   English Country Pottery 1950
Watney, B   English Blue and White Porcelain of the Eighteenth Century 1963
Fisher, S W   Worcester Porcelain 1970
Gilhespy, F B   Derby Porcelain 1961
Godden, G A   Lowestoft Porcelain 1969
          Coalport and Coalbrookdale Porcelains 1970
Lane, A   English Porcelain Figures of the 18th Century 1961
Mackenna, F S   Chelsea Porcelain, the Red Anchor Period 1951
          Chelsea Porcelain, the Gold Anchor Period 1952
Marshall, H R   Coloured Worcester Porcelain of the First Period 1964
Watney, B   Longton Hall Porcelain 1957

Cushion, J P, and Honey, W B   Handbook of Pottery and Porcelain Marks 1956
Fisher, S W   English Pottery and Porcelain Marks 1970
Godden, G A   Encyclopaedia of British Pottery and Porcelain Marks 1968

First published in USA in 1974
by Galahad Books, a division of
A & W Promotional Book Corp.
95 Madison Avenue, New York, NY 10016

© 1975 Octopus Books Ltd

ISBN 0 7064 0291 6

Produced by Mandarin Publishers Ltd
14 Westlands Road, Quarry Bay, Hong Kong

Printed in Hong Kong

Acknowledgments

The publishers would like to thank the following organizations and individuals for their kind permission to reproduce the pictures in this book:

John Bethell Photography 8 top, 10 top, 11, 12 left, 33 bottom
Antique Dealer and Collector's Guide 14, 28 bottom, 57 top & bottom, 71, 80–81
Connaissance des Arts 3, 28 top
Cooper-Bridgeman Library 33 top, 35, 36, 37 bottom, 39, 43 top, 47 top & bottom, 48, 49 top, 50 bottom, 55 top & bottom, 56 bottom, 58 top left, 62, 63, 65, 66 right, 69 top right, 70 top left & bottom, 73 top & bottom, 74 top, 75 top & bottom, 76 top & bottom, 77, 78, 79 top left, 80 top left, 81 top, 86, 87
Desmond Eyles 49 centre & bottom
A F Green 51, 56 top
Michael Holford Library 8, 15 top right, 18 top, 34 top right, 42, 79 right, 83 right
Angelo Hornak Photograph Library 44, 46, 59 top right
K Jung ZEFA 10 bottom
E Mariani ZEFA 6, 7
The Metropolitan Museum of Art 93, 94, 95
Musee des Arts Decoratifs, Paris 9 bottom
Musee Art Deco 16, 17, 18 bottom, 19 top, 21, 22, 23 top, 37 top, 52 bottom, 72 top
Museum Vandekar (Antique porcelain company) Front endpaper, 6–7, 12–13 top, 15 bottom, 20–21, 23 bottom, 24, 25, 27, 29, 30, 31 top, 31 bottom, 32, 38, 64 bottom, 67, 89 bottom
National Museum of Wales 60, 61, 82 top & bottom, 85 right
Anthony Oliver 59 bottom
Rockingham Museum 83 top left
Royal Doulton Tableware Ltd. 84, 85 bottom left
Snark International 9 bottom, 26, 34 top left
Sutton Antiques 58 bottom
Victoria & Albert Museum 13 right, 15 top left, 45 top & bottom, 66 left, 67, 80, 81
Wedgwood & Sons Ltd. 40, 41, 50 top, 53 top & bottom, 54 bottom right & left
Winifred Williams (Antiques) 43 bottom, 64 top, 68–69, 72 bottom, 74 bottom
Worcester Royal Porcelain Co. 88, 89 top, 92

FRONT ENDPAPER   *Spode tureen, cover and stand* period 1805–15

BACK ENDPAPER   *Dutch Delft garniture and butter-tubs* 18th century

CONTENT PAGE   *Bow frill vase* about 1760

TITLE PAGE   *Chinese famille rose wares* 18th century